TIME

The 100 Most Influential People Of All Time

Contents

Cornered *Pablo Picasso, photographed above in his home studio in Cannes in 1956, dominated 20th century art.* TIME *critic Robert Hughes called him "the Minotaur in a canvas-and-paper labyrinth of his own construction"*

Introduction

The Game-Changers

By Douglas Brinkley

JUST IMAGINE HOW HARD—OR WAS IT EASY?— for the TIME editorial team to decide who the 100 most influential people of all time were. Some of the figures, like Jesus Christ and Buddha, were self-evident. But how do you determine that Louis Armstrong is more significant than Duke Ellington? Or that Steve Jobs is more revolutionary than Bill Gates? The answer is, gut instinct and a belly full of hubris. While such lists serve no essential high purpose and can sometimes distort the past, they're great fun to compile—and worth doing. Yet I suspect the TIME editors suffered from a singular anxiety, the kind that can paralyze you when you try to fall asleep at night or enjoy a popcorn movie: Which individuals to leave in the pantheon, and which to leave out? It may have been a happy burden, but it was a burden nevertheless.

I was asked by TIME's editors to serve as a quasi-ombudsman for this book. It's been a labor of love. There is extraordinary learning utility in these elegant pages. Somehow, by reading short essays about history's Top 100 movers-and-shakers, the reader feels as if he has a useful springboard for grappling with the past. Every page is reader-friendly. You can omnivorously read from cover to cover, randomly turn to a gripping page that seizes your interest or simply study the historic illustrations. And there's an intriguing teaser quality to this volume. It challenges us, with each page turn: Will I be familiar with the next figure I see? TIME has, in fact, especially stoked my personal curiosity about three brave legends of old: Hippocrates (master of medicine), Euclid (genius geometer) and Guglielmo Marconi (wireless wizard). Marconi is one of the volume's also-rans—but that just shows how high TIME set the bar.

Most of the faces in this handsomely illustrated book have long been familiar to me. But there are exceptions. I was completely ignorant of Ashoka the Great, Saladin and Andrea Palladio. Now I'm not. One of the great perks of reading this book was broadening my knowledge of such long-ago figures as Akbar the Great (the third ruler of India's Islamic Mughal dynasty) and Umar ibn al-Khattab (a caliph who succeeded Muhammad and fostered Islam's ascent across the Middle East).

On the European front, I was already pretty intellectually grounded. I know my Martin Luther, Napoleon Bonaparte and William Shakespeare. Before reading this book, if I were chosen for a *Jeopardy* competition, I'd have easily been able to answer "Who is Maximilien Robespierre?" if given the clue "The leader of the French Revolution of the 1790s." But that would have been the extent of my biographical knowledge bank about Robespierre the person. Now, at least, I know that Robespierre was an attorney from Arras, an admirer of Jean-Jacques Rousseau's who went from Jacobin reformer to revolutionary to dictator to victim of the guillotine *(Sic semper tyrannis)*. I feel a little more well rounded.

When I was gearing up to write this foreword, I dipped into all sorts of scholarly treatises on the heroic individuals who have been the drill sergeants in civilization's noble march forward from the Dark Ages. Some, including Thomas Carlyle's *On Heroes, Hero-Worship, and the Heroic in History,* failed to achieve liftoff for me. But I strongly recommend comparative mythologist Joseph Campbell's *The Hero with a Thousand Faces.* (Back in 2011, TIME selected the book as one of the 100 best and most influential books written in English since Henry Luce and Briton Hadden founded the magazine in 1923.)

Campbell suggests that all lasting global myths are historically durable because they employ a recurring basic structure, one that he labels the monomyth. Most of TIME's picks fall into Campbell's monomyth paradigm: "A hero ventures forth from the world of common day into a region of supernatural wonder: fabulous forces are there encountered and a decisive victory is won: the hero comes back from this mysterious adventure with the power to bestow boons on his fellow man." This parallels the legendmaking we do today with real-life heroes like Bob Dylan or Gabriel García Márquez.

Is there a better Exhibit A of hero worship in this crazy world than the four huge faces carved on Mount Rush-

Brinkley is a professor of history at Rice University and the author of several best-selling books. Cronkite, a biography of the legendary broadcast journalist, was published in May 2012.

more? (Three of them—Lincoln, Jefferson and Washington—have been chosen as TIME Top 100 figures.) Yet recent revelations about one of those three, Jefferson, remind us that ours is a tough age for sustainable heroes. We live in a celebrity-centric society in which we build heroes up just to knock them down. We like I-gotchas, blemishes and warts. We relish being reminded that today's POTUS will be tomorrow's ex-President, begging for funds from donors to build a library in towns like Independence and Simi Valley. More people know the phrase "How the mighty have fallen" than have read Emerson's *English Traits and Representative Men.*

In fact, villains are as essential to history as heroes. At least 10 of TIME's choices are indisputable scoundrels. It always pains me to see pictures of Adolf Hitler in color, reminding me that the Third Reich rose and fell in my parents' lifetimes. It's startling to think that such wholesale evil infected the American Century. And Genghis Khan is romanticized too much—though not in this book—for my liking; he was a murderous thug.

A part of me wishes TIME had selected the 100 greatest people in world history instead of the most influential. But such a candy-coated approach would, in the end, be a far less interesting intellectual exercise. Patting ourselves on the back has its limits. Practically speaking, it's hard to have F.D.R. and Churchill on a Top 100 list without explaining that their stouthearted promotion of global democracy was triggered by the totalitarianism of Hitler. In our own daily life, we suffer high priests and dictators alike.

That unusual color photo of Hitler highlights another aspect of this volume: even as it gives our history-pondering muscles a good workout, it offers a visual feast of the first order. The photos of Pablo Picasso, Sigmund Freud and the Beatles are stunning. It's fun to study the artistic detail in Marc Chagall's take on Moses parting the clouds and Isidore Patrois's crowded painting of Joan of Arc. There are thousands of George Washington images, but TIME chose the most apropos one—his life mask by Jean-Antoine Houdon—which captures the first President's gravitas, his implacability and his stony remoteness from matters of flesh and blood.

TIME's editors understand that the visual imagery of legendary leaders reveals something about the leaders themselves (and, by extension, ourselves). Study carefully the compelling photo of Mohandas Gandhi on page 90 to notice how the great Hindu leader's ascetic appearance sandals, *khadi* loincloth and walking stick— was part and parcel of his back-to-the-spinning-wheel message. Or note the confident tilt of F.D.R.'s cigarette holder in the marvelous photograph on page 88. There is a self-assuredness to F.D.R. that spells doom for Germany and Japan in World War II.

In this Facebook and Google age, citizens tend to turn themselves into their own self-styled heroes. Everyone's favorite biographer is the person in the mirror. Why offer garlands to others when you can adore the cult of self? Nevertheless, a lot of the titans of civilization continue to exert a powerful psychic sway on us in the 21st century. As TIME notes, more than 3 billion people are followers of Christ, while Buddha weighs in with 350 million. Those are big-time fan clubs. Indeed, for all the talk of social history and people's history, character matters: most Americans would prefer to read a smart biography of Lincoln than an economic analysis of foodstuffs or industrial capacity during the Civil War. It's not too farfetched to say that we're a biography-drunk society. The famous—whether good (John F. Kennedy) or evil (Lee Harvey Oswald)— seize our attention. For better and worse, history often resolves into the sharpest focus when viewed through the lens of personality.

So, enjoy the biographical morsels in these pages written by such fine scholars as Robert Hughes and Peter Gay. Learn a few crucial historical facts. Get inspired to research further those game-changers who raise your curiosity index the most. One can argue with TIME's choices—the editors hope you do—but their thinking is sound in tapping the most influential over the most admirable. I particularly liked Walter Isaacson's take on the Code Crackers, Francis Crick and James Watson. What a weird marvel: the greatest biological breakthrough since Darwin's survival of the fittest, the double-helix-shaped DNA molecule, which Isaacson calls "heredity's master switch," was simply announced (on Feb. 28, 1953) at the Eagle Pub in Cambridge, England, with scant fanfare. Powerful images like Watson and Crick laughing in a pub near Cambridge University over their historic achievement in genetic cartography will stay with me forever.

If asked to summarize why I enjoyed this book so much, my answer would be pretty simple: it made me want to read more. I've just purchased three books about DNA, thanks to the audacity of TIME. ∎

Beacons of

the Spirit

Forsaking the passions of politics and the lure of riches, they followed a quieter path, one charted by the call of the soul. They are the saints and prophets, whose realm is not of this world.

From left: Buddhist mandala, Tibet; Christ as the Good Shepherd, Roman fresco; Abraham and Isaac, Israel; Socrates, Roman sarcophagus

The Sacrifice of Abraham, by Lelio Orsi, 16th century

Abraham

Primal Patriarch: c. 2100-1500 B.C.

ABRAHAM IS NOT ONLY A GIANT of Judaism and the Old Testament; he is also honored by Christians and Muslims. On a par with Moses, St. Paul and the Prophet Muhammad, Abraham represents a revolution in thought. He is the Ur-monotheist, the first man in the Bible to abandon all he knows in order to choose the Lord, forging a compact with his single God that enriches and explains his life.

Abraham's existence has not been proved, but he was born, tradition holds, into a family that sold idols—a legend that emphasizes the polytheism his people embraced before his enlightenment. The stirring first words of the 12th chapter in the *Book of Genesis* are God's to him and are often referred to as the Call: "Go forth from your native land/ And from your father's house/ And I will make of you a great nation." Abraham was ill-suited to the task: he was a childless 75-year-old whose wife Sarah was past menopause. Yet he complied, and after he fathered a child by a surrogate wife, Hagar, Sarah became pregnant with Abraham's second son, Isaac. Then, in an unforgettable test of his faith, God directed Abraham to offer up "your son, your only one, whom you love," as a human sacrifice. With powerful obedience, Abraham commenced to comply on a mountain called Moriah. At the last instant, God sent an angel to stay the father's hand and renewed his pledge to make a great nation of Abraham's descendants.

Christianity accepts Abraham's story as part of the Old Testament and honors the patriarch in contexts ranging from the Roman Catholic Mass to a Protestant children's song. Islam also acknowledges the Torah narrative of his life but with significant changes and additions. The Koran portrays Abraham as the first man to make full surrender to Allah, and each of Islam's five repetitions of daily prayer ends with a reference to him. As a central figure of three religions, Abraham—and the unique new God he worshipped, the single Lord—changed the world.

Confucius

Moral Philosopher: 551-479 B.C.

CONFUCIANISM IS NOT A RELIGION but a philosophy, for it does not deal with theology or speculation. Its founder lived in a time of civil war, working as an adviser to governors, traveling from one small warring province to another, trying to find one that would make his strong moral principles the guiding policy of the state. Confucius reached his goal in a brief period of power as chief magistrate of Chung-tu when he was 52. So potent was his example that "he was the idol of the people and flew in songs through their mouths."

Confucius was an advocate of stern self-control, a moralist without asceticism, a reformer without fanaticism, a conservative without bigotry, a scholar without pedantry, a rugged individualist with a social conscience. He preached the golden rule and moderation in all things. But Confucianism's reverence for elders and love of tradition made the philosophy anathema to Mao Zedong, who managed to stamp out its influence—briefly. Today, Confucius is once again the lodestar of a striving, materialistic people: Chinese chopsticks seldom stray far from Confucianism's dish.

Buddha

The Enlightened One
c. 563-480 B.C.

IN THE BEGINNING THE BUDDHA found enlightenment underneath a bodhi tree, near what is now Nepal. A pampered Himalayan prince, Siddhartha Gautama frustrated his father's efforts to shield him from the sights of suffering and death. At age 29, he left his beautiful young wife and son to become a wandering holy man. For six years Gautama fed on seeds, grass, even dung. He wore a hair shirt, lay on thorns, slept among rotting corpses. Finally it dawned on him that, far from escaping from his body by torturing it in yogi fashion, he was in fact giving it more than its due. Meditating beneath the bodhi tree, he resolved not to move until he had attained "supreme enlightenment" and had found the key to liberate man from himself.

Finally, in a great mystic rapture that lasted 49 days, enlightenment was attained, and Gautama became the Buddha, or Enlightened One. He eventually formulated the Four Noble Truths that unite all Buddhists today: that life is full of suffering; that most of that suffering, including the fear of death, can be traced to "desire," the mind's habit of seeing everything through the prism of the self and its well-being; that this craving can be transcended, leading eventually to an exalted state of full enlightenment called Nirvana; and that the means to do that lies in the Eightfold Path of proper views, resolve, speech, action, livelihood, effort, mindfulness and concentration. From the beginning, Buddhism has embraced meditation as a tool of enlightenment.

The Buddha posited no creator God; no Jehovah, Jesus or Allah. Buddhism's truths are so distinct from the primary concerns of other faiths that some regard it as a philosophy rather than a religion. Calm and welcoming, Buddhism has benignly bent and become a part of all that it has met; today its adherents number some 350 million people worldwide—including the two saffron-robed monks at left, praying at a temple in Cambodia.

The Death of Socrates, by Jacques-Louis David, 1787

Greece's Gadfly: c. 469-399 B.C.

SOCRATES ISSUED ONE OF HISTO-
ory's great calls to action. "The
unexamined life is not worth living,"
he declared, urging each of us to a
deeper encounter with our world. His influence persists in the Socratic method, which
pursues truth by posing a series of questions
that gradually reveal the truth or falsity of
a proposition; once expanded, this process
became the scientific method.

An intellectual rascal, Socrates loved to
prick the pomposities of the powerful, and
he was a familiar and much loved figure in
Athens during the city-state's glory days. Yet,
improbably, he ended up a martyr, after a
lifetime devoted to the pursuit of truth and
virtue. The details of his trial and death were
captured by one of his worshipful young
acolytes, Plato. Written around 360 B.C.,
Plato's famous *Apology* recounts how Socrates
defended himself against charges that he was
corrupting Athens' youth and blaspheming
local gods with his radical philosophical

musings. As a witness to the trial, Plato
recalled that his mentor refused to express re-
gret for his provocative stances, even going so
far as to liken himself to a "gadfly" trying to
arouse a "lazy horse" (read: Athenian society).

But while Socrates' ideas would go on to
shape thousands of years of Western thought,
a jury of his peers remained unimpressed; the
sage, age 70, was found guilty and condemned
to die. His disciples urged him to escape into
exile, but Socrates refused and carried out
the court's decree by drinking a cup of poison
hemlock, as memorably depicted in the familiar painting above by Jacques-Louis David.

Socrates' defiant martyrdom and Plato's
eloquent account of it remain touchstones
in the story of civilization's journey toward
self-discovery, rational inquiry, free speech
and moral courage. "In its impact on the
minds and emotions of Western man,
[Socrates' death] is an event that can be
compared only to the Passion and death of
Jesus," TIME's John Elson declared in 1988.

Socrates

Seeker of the Ideal: c. 424-348 B.C.

PLATO IS THE MAIN COURSE IN the three-course intellectual feast of Greece's Classical period: he was a student of Socrates and a teacher of Aristotle. These wise men were present at the creation of the long history of Western thought—and the power of their ideas is such that they remain vital presences in our culture after the passage of 2,400 years.

Of the three, Plato is the most purely philosophical, his thoughts ranging along the ridgeline between the harsh realities of our daily existence and the glorious ideals that our minds are drawn to: truth and beauty, justice and virtue. This world, he argued, is only a poor reflection of a more perfect world of pure forms and ideals that we aspire to inhabit.

Born into a well-to-do family, Plato became a disciple of Socrates' in his youth, and his most important writings are his 36 Socratic dialogues, which capture the rich interrogation of life and the world practiced by Socrates and his students. Both Plato's *Apology,* the story of Socrates' trial and death, and his *Republic* are classics of philosophy. The latter work describes Plato's ideal government and includes his classic allegory of the cave, which depicts men as prisoners in a cave, who see only the shadows of reality rather than its essence. His greatest work may not have been a text but a school: he founded and ran the Academy, the archetype for all rigorous centers of learning that followed, where free inquiry is encouraged and celebrated.

Plato

The School of Plato, Roman mosaic depicting the Academy, 1st century A.D.

Sacrificial Savior
c. 7-2 B.C.—30-36 A.D.

CHRISTIANITY, ONE OF HUMANity's great religions, was founded on the life and teachings of an itinerant Jewish preacher, Jesus of Nazareth, whose followers call him by an honorific, Christ, indicating that he was the Messiah (Anointed One), foreseen by Jewish prophets as the savior of Israel. Christians believe that Christ was of dual nature, the Son of God who assumed human form and preached lessons of love, humility and charity while performing miracles that proved his divine nature, before he was put to death by a Roman court. Jesus willingly sacrificed himself, they assert, thus atoning for the sins that are innate in all human beings, only to rise from the dead on Easter Sunday and ascend back to heaven. Most Christians further believe that Christ will return to earth at some point to pass judgment on all souls, both living and dead.

Roman chroniclers paid little attention to the Crucifixion of one man in a small nation, Judaea, of their vast empire. But in the centuries following Christ's death, his message was spread by his disciples and their followers, gradually attracting more and more adherents. In Rome the Christians were persecuted as a forbidden sect, but their devotion flourished under fire, and in the 4th century A.D. the Roman Emperor Constantine embraced Christianity, giving the church the temporal power it would long exert and leading to the institution's corruption, division and reform.

Though Christ's impact is undeniable, his character is malleable, always shaped by the cultural lens through which it is viewed. The medieval church saw him as the ideal knight, and later as Christ the King—a notion that fit in nicely with the Vatican's temporal claims. Some have seen him as a socialist, others as an advocate for the poor. To Muslims he is one of the prophets. His appeal remains strong: in 2012, 3 billion of the planet's 7 billion inhabitants described themselves as his followers.

Sacred scenes *Four scenes from the life of Christ—his birth, triumphant entry into Jerusalem, Crucifixion and Resurrection—were painted by the Italian master Giotto in the 14th century*

Jesus Christ

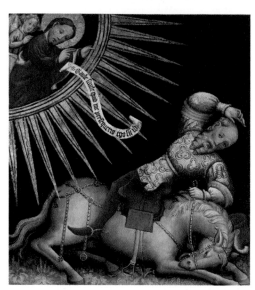

Conversion of St. Paul, German, 15th century

Charismatic Convert: c. A.D. 5-67

ST. PAUL THE APOSTLE WAS THE most effective, the most inspiring and the most widely traveled missionary in the early days of the Christian church. But this emblematic Apostle was not one of Christ's original 12 disciples: rather, Saul of Tarsus was a Jewish tentmaker and persecutor of Christ's early followers who underwent one of history's most famous religious conversions, when a vision of the resurrected Christ, cloaked in glory, is said to have blinded him as he rode from Jerusalem to Damascus.

Paul quickly became the most vigorous champion of the new religion, nourishing small communities of believers and sending them a series of powerful epistles that helped shape key tenets of the early church. He argued for the primacy of faith over good works in the pursuit of salvation, clarified the relations between the new laws of Christianity and the ancient laws of its predecessor religion, Judaism, and opened the church's doors to non-Jews. His views on the role of women in the church are not clear and remain controversial. Tradition holds that Paul was beheaded in Rome during the reign of Nero.

Muhammad

Prophet of Islam: c. 570-632

IN A CAVE AT THE FOOT OF MOUNT Hira near Mecca, where he had spent six months in solitary meditation, the vision came to Muhammad. The Angel Gabriel roused him from his bed with the stern command, repeated thrice, "Proclaim!" Thus it was, according to Islamic tradition, that an unremarkable Arab trader from Mecca was inspired to preach God's word in A.D. 610. Information about the life of the man who became known as the Messenger of Allah is relatively abundant, although the facts have been embellished with pious folklore.

The Prophet was born into a respected Meccan clan. Orphaned at 6, he was left in the care of a poor uncle and was set to work tending sheep. At 25, he married Khadijah, a rich Meccan widow, and began venturing into the desert to contemplate and pray. At 40, he began to preach his new faith; his revelations, as recorded by his adherents, were later collected as the Koran. In 622, after being harassed by his detractors, he and his followers fled to Medina in a migration known as the hegira. Six years later, he led his growing flock in a pilgrimage back to Mecca to visit the Kaaba, believed to be the spot where Abraham prepared to sacrifice his son Ishmael (as Islam teaches) at God's command. In 630 the Prophet led an army of 10,000 into his former city, taking control in a bloodless victory.

Following the death of its Prophet in 632, Islam spread rapidly across the Arab world, driven by its Five Pillars of practice: believing the creed; performing five prayers daily; giving alms; fasting during Ramadan; and making a pilgrimage to Mecca at least once in a lifetime. Civilization's youngest major religion is now its second largest faith and claims 1.5 billion believers across the globe.

Resting place *Pilgrims pray at Medina's Mosque of the Prophet, burial site of Islam's founder, in December 2006. The mosque is the religion's second holiest site, after the Kaaba in Mecca*

Scholar, Sage, Physician: 1135-1204

RELIGIOUS SAGE, PHILOSOPHER, rabbi, community leader and physician, Moses ben Maimon was also culturally complex: a Jew steeped in ancient Greek philosophy, he spent his life among Muslims and exerted a strong influence on Christian Europe. As a Russian scholar noted, "Maimonides is perhaps the only philosopher in the Middle Ages ... who symbolizes a confluence of four cultures: Greco-Roman, Arab, Jewish and Western."

Muslim scholars regard Maimonides foremost as an Islamic thinker, yet he is also highly esteemed by Orthodox Jews, who frequently quote his sayings and avidly study the Mishnah Torah, his magisterial commentary on parts of the Talmud. His philosophical masterpiece, *The Guide For the Perplexed,* continues to inspire more secularized Jews and many other readers.

Maimonides was born in the Spanish city of Córdoba; he was 13 when the Almohad, a fanatical Muslim movement, seized control of his hometown and gave Jews the choice of death, conversion or exile. The Maimon family, choosing to depart, wandered for a decade before settling in Fez, then the capital of Morocco. Maimonides, educated by his father and other local rabbis, soon began his writings, which contain the 13 Principles of Faith, to this day part of synagogue ritual. In 1166 he moved to his final refuge, Egypt, after persecution of the Jews reached Morocco. There he wrote the Mishnah Torah, whose preface contains what became Judaism's standard listing of the 613 biblical commandments. He also became the physician to the court of the Sultan Saladin and wrote copious works on medicine that strongly influenced Christian scholars and physicians in the Middle Ages.

Native son *A statue honors Maimonides in the Jewish quarter in Córdoba, Spain, his hometown*

Jalaluddin Rumi

Spin zone *Turkey's spiritual order, the Whirling Dervishes, right, was founded by followers of Rumi, left*

Mystic Poet: 1207-73

JALALUDDIN RUMI WAS, AMONG many other things, a lover of irony. So he might have savored the fact that, though his poems are deeply Islamic, Madonna has set translations of his 13th century verses praising Allah to music; that Donna Karan has used recitations of them at her fashion shows; and that both *The Essential Rumi,* published in 1995, and *The Soul of Rumi,* published in 2001, have been wildly successful with U. S. readers.

Born in today's Afghanistan, Rumi spent most of his younger years as a refugee—on the run from Genghis Khan to his east and the Crusaders to the west. The son of a scholar, Rumi set out to become one himself, but spiritually, he was hungry for something more—something that came to him in 1244, when he met a ragged, wild-eyed mystic named Shams of Tabriz. The meeting transformed the young Persian intellectual into a mystic, but he was shattered when Shams was murdered. After a long period of mourning, Rumi experienced another mystical intuition: Shams was within him in spiritual form.

Now Rumi's formidable output of poetry began. His masterpiece, the *Masnavi,* is a fantastical, oceanic mishmash of folktales, philosophical speculation and lyric ebullience that has strongly influenced the music, writing and culture of a large swath of the Middle East. His writings have attracted millions of Muslims to Sufism, Islam's mystical branch.

Coleman Barks, a poet and retired professor at the University of Georgia, is responsible for Rumi's new popularity in the U.S. His inspired, free hand with the Sufi master's works has won them a deserved new following, if at the expense of glancing over the poet's intensely personal engagement with Islam, which is at their core. For novices, even Rumi Lite is better than no Rumi at all.

St. Francis of Assisi

Humble Spirit: 1182-1226

FRANCESCO DI BERNADONE WAS born into a prosperous Italian family at a time of European plenty. To encourage riches, the Roman Catholic church preached industry, a get-ahead attitude that had little regard for outcasts, for lepers, for the poor. The revelation of Francis—and apparently it was a revelation, a life-changing event—was that poverty was holy and that the human spirit approached God when in want. The wealthy aristocrat of Assisi soon startled his friends and family by kissing lepers and giving away his fine clothes and possessions. He joined the supplicants outside St. Peter's Basilica in Rome, then founded an order of humble friars who begged for their daily bread, inspiring many followers to join him.

An ecstatic spirit deeply attuned to the beauty of nature, Francis saw animals as fellow creatures of God; he is famously said to have preached to the birds, as shown in the painting at left, modeled on a work by Giotto. He employed animals when he became the first person to celebrate Christmas by re-creating the scene at the manger in Bethlehem when Christ was born, handing down a tradition still practiced around the world. Yet though he exalted nature, he treated his body with contempt, seeing it only as a home for the spirit. Late in life he experienced stigmata, the ultimate sign of grace earned through suffering, bleeding from five wounds similar to those suffered by Christ on the cross.

Saints make for poor followers, and the leaders of the church correctly saw Francis' ministry as a direct threat to their authority. They undermined his teachings by co-opting his Franciscan order, which gorged itself with power and wealth after the founder's death.

A saint for all seasons and all ages, Francis became an icon to idealistic youths in the 1960s who venerated his poverty and humility, his joyous bond with nature and animals. He was celebrated in folk songs, in an overwrought Franco Zeffirelli movie, in a powerful novel by Nikos Kazantzakis. In today's sterner times, he remains a quiet presence in many lives, a stone figure hidden amid the greenery in thousands of gardens around the world.

Deep Thinker: 1724-1804

AS THE ENLIGHTENMENT MOVED like an electric current through the world of the 18th century, it left in its wake the scorched husks of customs, religions and philosophies that no longer seemed tenable in a post-Newtonian world. Wielding doubt and skepticism like battering rams, scientists and philosophers challenged so many of the fundamental beliefs that had kept society ticking along for centuries that it sometimes seemed as if they had left themselves without solid ground to stand on. Immanuel Kant, the son of simple tradespeople in Königsberg, East Prussia (now Kaliningrad in Russia), created a new way to resolve the contradictions wrought by the advance of science.

Philosophers and scientists in Kant's day were deeply divided. The empiricists believed that experience is the ultimate source of knowledge, while rationalists maintained that some knowledge of the world outside us can be gained independently of sense experience. In his *Critique of Pure Reason* (1781) and many other influential works, Kant found common ground between the two schools of thought, arguing that while experience is fundamentally necessary for human knowledge, reason is necessary for processing that experience into coherent thought. He thus argues for the primacy of the human mind, even as he admits its limitations.

Immanuel Kant

Icon *Mother Teresa in Calcutta in her later years*

Saint of the Gutters: 1910-97

LIKE HER SAINTLY PREDECESSOR, Francis of Assisi, she led by example, and her good works became so well known that her iconic white garb with its blue trim is now equated with her ideals of service and charity among "the poorest of the poor." She was born Agnes Bojaxhiu to Albanian parents living under the Ottoman Empire. When she was 7, her father was murdered. Bojaxhiu chose emigration over political activism, and at the age of 18 she entered the Sisters of Loreto's convent in Ireland as a novice. The missionary teaching order sent her to Bengal in 1929.

After 17 years as a teacher in Calcutta (Kolkata), the nun, then 36, took a 400-mile (645 km) train trip to Darjeeling. She had been working herself sick, and her superiors ordered her to relax during a retreat in the Himalayan foothills. On the ride out, she later reported, Christ spoke to her. He called her to abandon teaching and work instead in "the slums" of the city, dealing directly with "the poorest of the poor"—the sick, the dying, beggars and street children. "Come, come,

carry Me into the holes of the poor," he told her. "Come be My light."

The petite nun left her order and founded a new missionary community of 13 members. That small order eventually grew into a global network of more than 4,000 sisters running orphanages and AIDS hospices. Her fame spread, and in 1979 "the Saint of the Gutters" was awarded the Nobel Peace Prize.

Some skeptics have painted her as fame-hungry or sanctimonious, while a 2007 TIME cover story revealed that Mother Teresa suffered deep crises of faith, in which her belief in the value of her work, even her faith in God, deserted her. Others criticized her for lacking adequate medical training, for not addressing poverty on a grander scale, for actively opposing birth control and abortion and even for cozying up to dictators. But for every doubter there were many more admirers: the radiant example of her self-abnegating service lit up the world like a beacon, inspiring countless volunteers to serve, and there is little doubt that Mother Teresa will wear her blue-and-white sari all the way to Catholic sainthood.

Other Exemplars of the Spirit
Three driven missionaries carried their message to the world

Lao Tzu
c. 6th century B.C.
The name by which history knows him, Lao Tzu (or Laozi), is an honorific; the given name of this influential Chinese holy man is Li Er. He is said to have lived at the time of Confucius or slightly before that equally significant Chinese philosopher. As is the case with Homer, Abraham and Moses, many modern scholars maintain that Lao Tzu is a legendary character whose life story exemplifies the doctrines of his religion, Taoism.

Confucius concerned himself with worldly affairs; Lao Tzu, in contrast was a mystic whose masterwork, the *Tao Te Ching,* is a vast treatise of axioms, adages, learning and moral strictures, all flowing from a belief that the guiding spirit of Tao (pronounced *daow*) flows in and around all living things. The *Tao* encourages people to act in accordance with this positive spiritual energy; to divert from this path is to embrace wickedness and sin. Unlike Confucius, Lao Tzu is regarded as a divine being by his most ardent followers.

St. Augustine
354-430
The clever young North African, 32, was a teacher of rhetoric who had been drawn toward Christianity but enjoyed the company of women too much to pursue religion. Then, in 386 A.D., he heard a child's voice chanting, *"Tolle lege, tolle lege"* (Take up and read, take up and read). Snatching the Bible, he read Paul's admonition in Romans 13 to abandon wanton living and "put on the Lord Jesus Christ"—and did so.

As Bishop of Hippo, he preached daily for 35 years and wrote copiously on doctrine. Long before Calvin, Augustine championed predestination; before Luther, he taught salvation by God's grace, not by good works. He helped define church teaching on the Trinity, conditions for waging a "just war" and the "original sin" that corrupts all humanity. *The Confessions,* his masterpiece, is a pioneering autobiography and a forerunner of modern psychology. In Pope John Paul II's words, Augustine is the "common father of our Christian civilization."

Pope John Paul II
1920-2005
The ascension to the papacy of a Roman Catholic Cardinal from the Soviet-dominated nation of Poland at the height of the cold war in 1978 was so unexpected that many still regard the event as divinely guided. Taking the name John Paul II in honor of his predecessor, who died after serving only 33 days in office, Karol Cardinal Wojtyla, who had lived through the occupation of his nation by both Germans and Russians, became the first non-Italian Pope in 455 years.

As Pope, John Paul marshaled his beaming smile and common touch to become the most charismatic Pontiff in centuries. Although church liberals decried his conservative bent in doctrinal matters, John Paul revived his church, took its message memorably to millions, honored other religions and helped lead Poland from Soviet domination. Currently on a fast-track to sainthood, he remains admired by millions who do not share his faith.

Explorers and

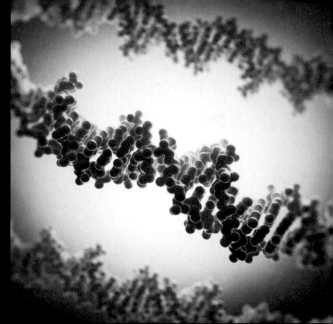

Visionaries

Some set out to chart and understand their world. Others dreamed of things that had never existed, then crafted them. All plunged into realms unknown: they are the pioneers.

From left: Isaac Newton's telescope; *Darwin's Finches*, by John Gould; world map, 15th century Catalan; human DNA, illustration

Hippocrates

MODERN MEDICINE HAS GROWN by means of a tradition that is almost 2,400 years old. Its practices are said to have begun on the Greek island of Kos, near the western coast of Asia Minor, where a school arose around the teachings of the legendary physician Hippocrates. Today the name of Hippocrates is mentioned most frequently in discussions of the oath attributed to him, still taken by beginning physicians. In one of history's longest chains of ethics, today's physicians still swear by the code of Hippocrates, pledging to do no harm and to maintain the privacy of their patients. But the followers of Hippocrates did far more than introduce the principles from which the codes of today's medical ethics have developed.

Perhaps the single most striking difference between the doctors of the Hippocratic school and all others was their injunction that the causes of disease should no longer be attributed to the influence of supernatural forces. Henceforth, the origins of illness were to be sought in observable natural factors that influence the functions of the body. Attempts were made to relate specific symptoms to actual internal or environmental causes, rather than to the intervention of displeased and vengeful gods. This was a departure for physicians accustomed to seeking cures by appealing to the divinities with prayer and sacrifice.

Casting off the shroud of mysticism, the Greek physicians replaced it with the thesis that the causes and cures of every disease are not only quite natural but also discoverable through the careful study of each patient. Thus curiosity, keenness of observation and the value of scrupulous record keeping became paramount priorities in the new philosophy of care. And as knowledge grew and was shared within the guild, the experience of a single physician became the experience of all.

Over the course of several hundred years, a literature, later known as the Hippocratic Corpus, was created, forming the basis of all medical practice. Since that time, the accumulated and recorded knowledge of one generation has been passed on to the next through literature and via those who teach their successors. *Docere,* the Latin word from which the word doctor is derived, means "to teach."

—*By Sherwin B. Nuland*

Euclid

Geometry's Genius: c. 325-265 B.C.

LITTLE IS KNOWN OF THE LIFE OF Euclid, but the Greek mathematician who is believed to have lived in the great Egyptian center of Hellenistic learning, Alexandria, needed only his work to stamp his mark on history. Euclid, like Newton and Einstein, ranks among history's great diviners of nature's rules and regulations. He not only found, described and defined the mathematical relationships that govern the shapes we encounter in nature, but he also devised the set of tools with which succeeding generations could further his work.

Euclid's basic findings are set forth in his *Elements,* an introduction to geometry and mathematical theory that is considered to be among the most translated, published and studied works in the history of Western culture (and perhaps among the most cursed by young students). Preserved by Arab scholars during Europe's Dark Ages, this classic text was the primary source for geometric reasoning, theorems and methods from the time of Alexander the Great to the 19th century, when new directions began to emerge—a development so unexpected that the advanced schools of thought were defined in the negative, as non-Euclidean geometry. In addition to his pioneering work in mathematics and geometry, Euclid is regarded as one of the fathers of deductive reasoning, and thus of the scientific method.

Father of Invention: 287-212 B.C.

Archimedes

A POLYMATH WHOSE BRILLIANT insights into the workings of nature led to fundamental theories in physics, mathematics and geometry, Archimedes wasn't like Albert Einstein, who revolutionized our understanding of the universe through "thought experiments" conducted only in his head. The Greek scientist, born in Syracuse, was a hands-on genius who excelled as an engineer and an inventor. According to ancient texts, Archimedes helped defend Syracuse from a Roman armada by using a lens to magnify the rays of the sun and set enemy boats on fire. Modern scientists believe that the basics of the story may be true, but that Archimedes most likely started the fire by using the polished shields of massed soldiers to reflect the sun's rays onto a ship; TIME reported on a successful attempt to replicate the feat in 1973, but two more recent attempts, on the TV series *Mythbusters,* failed.

Archimedes gave science its defining image: the genius supposedly leaped from his bath, shouting "Eureka!" ("I have found it!"), after realizing that the volume of solids could be measured by placing them in water. He also invented the Archimedean screw, a mechanism used by the ancients to pump bilge water from ships. His work with the power of levers made him declare, "Give me a place to stand and I will move the earth." And move it he did.

Aristotle

Passionate Polymath
384-322 B.C.

Aristotle with a Bust of Homer, by Rembrandt van Rijn, 1653

HE WAS A RENAISSANCE MAN 16 centuries before the Italian Renaissance began. Aristotle lived in the glory days of Classical Greece; born in Stagirus in the colony of Chalcidice in the north of Greece, he found his way to Athens as a young man, where he studied with the finest of teachers, Plato, at the original Academy. Aristotle lingered there for 20 years, leaving when he was not chosen to lead the celebrated center of learning after Plato's death. When Aristotle in turn became a teacher, he taught the finest of students: Alexander, son of King Philip II of Macedon. It was Aristotle who suggested to his student that he turn his dreams to the east, laying out the path of conquest that would earn the prince his defining sobriquet, "the Great."

Aristotle will forever be associated with Plato and Plato's teacher, Socrates; linked in our minds as a power trio of Greek philosophers, they can seem indistinguishable. But the detail from Raphael's painting at left, *The School of Athens* (1510-11), suggests their differences. Plato, on the left, was primarily a philosopher, pointing to the heavens as he sought life's absolutes, while Aristotle's posture suggests his eagerness to encounter the world and take its measure by gathering, dissecting, studying and classifying nature's abundance: he was as much scientist as philosopher. The titles of his most famous treatises reveal the panoramic range of his interests: *Politics, Physics, Metaphysics, De Anima* (On the Soul), *Nicomachean Ethics* and *Poetics*. Even that list excludes his investigations into zoology, biology, logic, astronomy, anatomy, geology, meteorology and a host of other disciplines. His gaze was restless, analytical, rigorous—and it fell everywhere. He is regarded as the father of deductive reasoning and the formal science of logic.

After leaving the Academy circa 348 B.C., Aristotle traveled in Asia Minor and to the island of Lesbos, collecting botanical, zoological and geological samples. He served as head of the royal academy in Macedonia and Alexander's tutor for several years, beginning in 343 B.C., but by 335 B.C. he had returned to Athens, where he founded his own academy, the Lyceum. He composed most of his works in the years that followed, although, according to ancient texts, perhaps two-thirds of his works have been lost, to civilization's great detriment.

Aristotle's past caught up with him as Alexander's empire grew. Aristotle took issue with his erstwhile student's proclamation that he was divine, which may have been a concession to his conquered peoples, who sought divinity in their rulers. A paranoid Alexander responded by threatening Aristotle in letters. After Alexander's death in 323 B.C., Athens turned against Macedon. The city was no place for Alexander's tutor, and Aristotle fled to northwest Greece, where he died at age 62.

Muhammad ibn Musa al-Khwarizmi

Algebra's Father: 780-850

OF ALL HISTORY'S MISNOMERS, perhaps none has distorted our view of the past as effectively as the name long given to the period between the fall of Rome and the emergence of the medieval world: the Dark Ages. Yes, those centuries were challenging for many in Europe, but even as the Christian West declined, the Arab world, afire with the new religion of Islam, reached magnificent heights of cultural and artistic achievement.

In the 9th century A.D., Baghdad was the most dazzling city in the world and a center of great learning. Here two Caliphs, Harun al-Rashid and his son al-Ma'mun, nurtured the House of Wisdom, where scholars translated the great works of Greece and Persia into Arabic, and astronomers, mathematicians, physicians and other scientists made significant contributions to world culture. Among them was al-Khwarizmi, a Persian scholar who introduced the decimal system to the West and pioneered the use of quadratic equations. Never heard of this genius? Yes, you have: his name is embedded in English as the words *algebra* and *algorithm,* each a form of the mathematician's name transliterated into Latin.

First class *The U.S.S.R. observed the scholar's 1,200th birthday on a postage stamp in the 1980s*

Zheng He

Bold Navigator: c. 1371-1433

THE ACHIEVEMENTS OF ZHENG He, China's Muslim eunuch admiral of the 15th century, are on a par with those of Columbus, Da Gama and Magellan. Yet for long centuries his accomplishments languished, forgotten. Now, as a resurgent China reaches out to the world, the great navigator and explorer has found new favor in Beijing and new respect abroad.

In 2005, China marked with nationwide celebrations the 600th anniversary of the seven voyages, undertaken by Zheng's vast "treasure fleets" from 1405 to 1433; the opening ceremony of the 2008 Olympic Games in Beijing dramatized his explorations from Southeast Asia to the Middle East and the shores of eastern Africa. In 2010, Chinese officials announced Beijing was funding a three-year project with the assistance of the Kenyan government to search for vessels of Zheng's large fleets that are thought to have foundered off the East African coast.

Zheng's unprecedented display of maritime power was meant to extend the Ming dynasty's reach over a network of tributary states. Yet, as Chinese scholars like to point out, the admiral rarely resorted to the type of violent coercion employed by European colonizers. Muslim scholars note that Zheng practiced Islam, as did Ma Huan, the main chronicler aboard the ships. It's likely they were guided to their many ports of call, such as Melaka, India's Malabar Coast and Malindi in Kenya, by Muslim pilots of Arab, Indian or African extraction. But Zheng's great discoveries, like those of the Norse explorer Leif Ericsson, were never repeated, and the door closed on China's expansive era.

Navigator *A 16th century Chinese manuscript shows Zheng in command of one of his armadas*

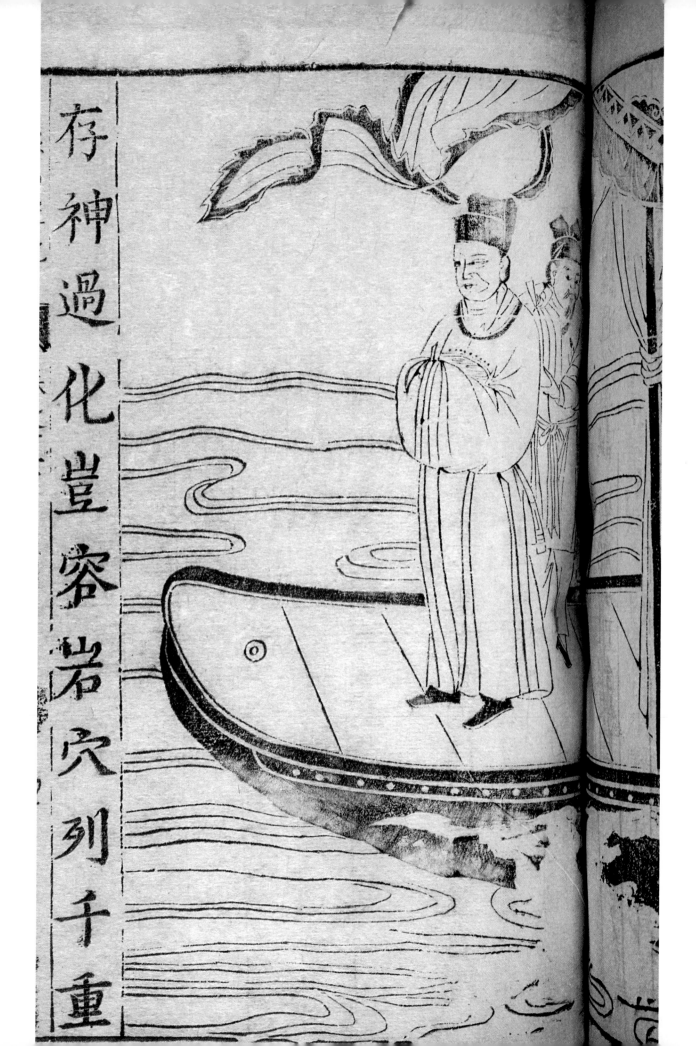

存神過化豈容岩穴列千重

Nicolaus Copernicus

EVEN IN A BOOK DEVOTED TO THE 100 people who have most moved the world, it's rare to meet an individual who accomplished just that. But with the publication of his magnum opus, *De Revolutionibus Orbium Coelestium* (On the Revolution of the Heavenly Spheres), in 1543, Nicolaus Copernicus forever changed our view of the earth's place in the cosmos. His breakthrough heliocentric theory, which posits that our planet revolves around the sun, replaced the geocentric model developed by the Roman scientist Ptolemy, which had prevailed for some 1,300 years, in which the earth is the center of the cosmos. The Polish astronomer's brilliant insights on the revolutions of heavenly bodies in turn sparked a revolution on this planet, where his theory was rebuked by leaders of the Roman Catholic Church, even as it helped ignite a surging new interest in the scientific method as a powerful tool of illumination and progress.

Copernicus, a child of the Renaissance, traveled across Europe to study with the greatest scholars of the age. After attending classes at Cracow University (now Jagiellonian University), he traveled to one of the age's bustling new hives of inquiry, the University of Bologna. There he studied for four years with the great scholars of his time while devouring the works of Greek and Roman scientists, many only newly available in Western Europe. After studying medicine at the University of Padua, Copernicus returned to Poland in 1503 at age 30, where he spent most of his remaining years refining his paradigm-shattering view of the cosmos, which he had already begun developing.

If a pioneer in science, Copernicus was a religious man who took minor orders in the Catholic church and from 1512 served as canon of the cathedral in Frombork on Poland's Baltic coast, where he made astronomical

Nicolaus Copernicus, Artist unknown, 1575

observations with rudimentary equipment. In one of history's great death scenes—it is perhaps apocryphal—he was handed the first copy of his masterwork after waking from a coma on the day he died, May 24, 1543.

Initial reaction to his theory was mild, but outrage grew and the church eventually banned his work until 1835. A fellow Jagiellonian University student, Pope John Paul II, visited Copernicus' birthplace, Torun, in 1999 and hailed the achievements of his countryman. In 2005, after years of searching, Copernicus' remains were identified when a tooth from a skull in a grave beneath an altar in Frombork Cathedral was found to match the DNA of two strands of hair tucked in a book the astronomer once owned. Somewhere, one hopes, the visionary scientist was smiling.

Christopher Columbus

Intrepid Navigator: 1451-1506

COLUMBUS' STORY COMES TO us with a number of apocrypha patched onto the figure of the Discoverer, as the 19th century called him. Some are obviously false, such as the tenacious tale that Queen Isabella sold her jewels to pay for his first voyage to the Americas, or that the *Santa Maria* was crewed by convicts, or that Columbus was trying to prove the world was round. (No educated person in the late 15th century, and no mariner either, believed otherwise.) He has been presented as Castilian, Catalan, Corsican, Majorcan, Portuguese, French, English, Greek and even Armenian. He was, in fact, Italian: born in Genoa, the son of a weaver.

Columbus' sense of his humble origins was crucial. He was determined to transcend them; his means would be navigation. At first he wanted to succeed through trade. As a merchant navigator, he sailed all over the Mediterranean, to the Guinea coast of Africa and as far north as Ireland. Sometime between 1478 and 1484, the full plan of self-aggrandizement and discovery took shape in his mind. He would win glory, riches and a title of nobility by opening a trade route to the untapped wealth of the Orient. No reward could be too great for the man who did that.

This drive is one of the few attributes of Columbus that all the surviving sources agree on. It was clear to the crew of the *Santa Maria* as the little fleet was pitching and rolling west in 1492, with no land yet in sight and mutiny brewing. He could be extremely petty, and his reports to the crown were absurdly self-serving. Yet the achievement of his first voyage in 1492 remains: he opened a route to the New World that could be sailed again, by himself and others, over and over—and was. He united the western and eastern hemispheres of the world across the Atlantic. No man had done so before.

—*By Robert Hughes*

Incoming *This colorized version of an engraving by Theodore de Bry, a noted 16th century illustrator of the Age of Discovery, depicts Columbus landing at Hispaniola in December 1492*

Ferdinand Magellan, Artist unknown, 16th century

Global Voyager: 1480-1521

THE IMPORT OF MAGELLAN'S signal achievement is beyond doubt: he was the leader of the first expedition that circumnavigated the globe, a three-year voyage biographer Stefan Zweig describes as "the most glorious Odyssey in the history of mankind." The Portuguese admiral, funded by the King of Spain, was the first to sail from the Pacific Ocean to the Atlantic via the strait below South America that now bears his name. He was also the first European mariner to cross the Pacific.

Yet the man's character remains elusive: he is often portrayed as a cold-blooded martinet, a double-crosser who aimed to betray Spain and set up in the king business in the East Indies. But Zweig, for one, while conceding Magellan was a secretive, unpersonable dictator, defends him as a sincere man whose ruthlessness was an unavoidable means toward a great end.

The great voyage, which left Spain with five ships on Sept. 20, 1519, was a catalog of atrocities: when mutiny broke out in Argentina, Magellan had its leaders drawn and quartered or simply marooned. Magellan himself met his end in the Philippines, killed by natives when he took sides in a local rivalry. The remnant of Magellan's expedition arrived back in Spain on Sept. 6, 1522: one ship and 18 men of the 270 who had left almost exactly three years before. Of such horrors are glorious Odysseys made.

Ferdinand Magellan

Johannes Gutenberg, by Jean Antoine Laurent, 1831

Information's Liberator: c. 1395-1468

YOU SAY YOU WANT A REVOLU-
ion? In the 15th century an obscure
German printer kindled religious
rebellions and transformed the
social order by inventing a new technology:
printing with movable metal type. Johannes
Gutenberg was born to well-to-do parents in
Mainz. Details of his life, early as well as late,
are sketchy, but he apparently trained as a
goldsmith and/or gemcutter and then became
a partner in a printing shop in Strasbourg.

At the time, printing was a laborious
process that used incised blocks of wood as
printing forms. Gutenberg explored using
metal casts of the individual letters of the
alphabet, letters he could use and reuse in any
order. There were technical obstacles: he had
to find a metal alloy that would melt at mod-
erate temperatures, so that it could be poured
into letter molds, as well as an ink that would
crisply transfer impressions from metal to
paper. He adapted a wine press to provide the
force that bonded the ink to the paper.

In 1455 visitors to the Frankfurt Trade Fair
reported having seen a marvel: sections
of a Latin Bible with two columns of 42
lines apiece cleanly printed on each page.
The completed book appeared about a year
later; it did not bear its printer's name, but it
eventually became known as the Gutenberg
Bible. Just as it was released, Gutenberg was
forced to turn over his shop and some of his
equipment to one of his investors. But the
technology he had created spread quickly
across Europe.

By 1500, within five decades, an estimated
30,000 titles had been published. The result
was an unprecedented explosion of knowledge. The dissemination of Greek and Roman
texts helped spark the Renaissance. Printed
religious texts removed the grip of clerical
middlemen on sacred texts and led to an
emphasis on personal salvation that helped
fuel the Protestant Reformation. As literacy
spread, in the greatest extension of human
consciousness ever created, aging hierarchies
toppled. Gutenberg had launched a new kind
of revolution—an information revolution.

Cosmic Columbus: 1564-1642

IF ANY ONE MAN LAID THE FOUNDA-tion of modern science, it was Galileo Galilei of Pisa. Gifted in mathematics and astronomy, he discovered the laws of falling bodies and, legend has it, proved them by dropping objects from the top of a handy, if unorthodox, scientific instrument: his city's famed Leaning Tower.

Galileo calculated the parabolic motion of projectiles, described the motion of objects rolling down an inclined plane and invented a military compass and the pendulum clock, among many other achievements. But his reputation as one of nature's great explorers rests upon his breakthroughs in astronomy. Hearing in 1609 that a spyglass had been invented in Holland, he built one of his own, turned it on the heavens and in short order

discovered, and confirmed in his writings, that four large moons were orbiting Jupiter, that Venus had phases and that the sun had spots—all of which, to his grave misfortune, contradicted Roman Catholic Church dogma.

The universe, Galileo insisted, "is written in the language of mathematics … without which … one is wandering about in a dark labyrinth." For Galileo's sins, which included his adherence to the Copernican view that the earth revolves around the sun, the Inquisition in 1633 condemned him, compelled him to abjure his findings and placed him under permanent house arrest, where he remained until his death. Three hundred years later, the church emerged from its sojourn in the dark labyrinth and conceded Galileo had been right all along.

Galileo Galilei, by Felix Farra, 1873

René Descartes, by Sébastien Bourdon, c. 1630-45

Cogitator: 1596-1650

RENE DESCARTES SUMMED UP HIS philosophy in three elegant words: *Cogito, ergo sum:* I think, therefore I am. From this simple statement flowed an entire system of thought. Descartes was a master of systems; like Aristotle, he was both an eminent scientist and a groundbreaking philosopher. Often described as the first modern philosopher, this man of bifocal vision posited humans themselves as creatures of duality, and he enshrined this metaphysical divide in what came to be known in Western philosophy as mind-body dualism. The psychic space inside our heads is infinite and ethereal, he argued; it seems obvious that it must be made of different stuff than all the other organs. Love and anger, he noted, can't be collected in a test tube to be weighed and measured. Eastern philosophy, in contrast, posits that mind and body belong to an indivisible continuum, a view increasingly validated by modern Western science.

Descartes's achievements in science are less fungible: the Frenchman who spent his creative years in the Netherlands left an enduring mark in mathematics as a pioneer of analytical geometry and calculus. A champion of observation, deduction and reason, he is one of the founders of the scientific method—and had his works banned by the church as a result.

Cosmic Calculator: 1642-1727

THE FIRST OF HIS FAMILY of Lincolnshire yeomen to be able to write his name, Isaac Newton grew into a touchy, passionately focused introvert who could go without sleep for days. At a highly precocious age, he absorbed everything important that was known to science up to that time. Riding on the shoulders of giants, he began assembling the Newtonian universe, a miraculously predictable and rational clockwork creation held together by a universal force of gravitation and regulated by his elegant laws of motion.

The bulk of Newton's formative thought was achieved at ages 23 and 24, while the Great Plague halted his studies at Cambridge University. Before his death at 84, he had set off four scientific revolutions: in mathematics (he co-invented the calculus), in optics (he invented the reflecting telescope, and he established the nature of color and the components of sunlight), in mechanics (his three laws of motion changed the world) and with his theory of gravity, which explained the phenomena of heaven and earth in a single mathematical system—or did until Einstein upset the applecart.

—*By Lance Morrow*

Isaac Newton, by James Thornhill, 1710

Meriwether Lewis: 1774-1809
William Clark: 1770-1838
Sacagawea: c. 1788-1812

WHEN PRESIDENT THOMAS JEF-ferson sent Meriwether Lewis, William Clark and a company of men up the Missouri River and into the terra incognita of the lands newly acquired in the Louisiana Purchase, the young United States already had a Constitution, but it lacked an epic vision. It had a government but no real identity. Lewis, Clark and their Corps of Discovery helped invent one—with the essential assistance of a young Indian woman, Sacagawea.

The Native American, pregnant at 16, was the wife of Toussaint Charbonneau, a fur trapper serving the expedition as a guide; she was valued for her knowledge of the Shoshone language. Clark helped her give birth inside a wintry fort, and she repaid him a thousand times over by arranging with her Indian kinsmen for the expedition's safe passage over the Rockies. As Clark noted in his diary, "The sight of this Indian woman … confirmed those people of our friendly intentions."

Lewis and Clark kept perhaps the most complete journals in the history of human exploration (some of which survived only because Sacagawea jumped into a stream to retrieve them when a canoe capsized). We can look over their shoulders as they and their party contend with hunger, disease, blizzards, broiling sun, boiling rapids, furious grizzly bears and plagues of "musquetors." When their party returned to St. Louis after 26 months on the road, the blank spaces on the American map had been filled in—and the nation's continental destiny beckoned.

Charles Darwin

Galapagos tortoises (*Geochelone nigra*), Galápagos Islands

CHARLES DARWIN DIDN'T WANT to murder God, as he once put it. He didn't want to defy his fellow Cantabrigians, his gentlemanly Victorian society, his devout wife. But he did. He waited 20 years to publish his theory of natural selection, but—fittingly, after another scientist threatened to be first—he finally did.

Before Darwin, most people accepted some version of biblical creation. Humans were seen as the pinnacle of godly architecture. But the young biologist's five-year voyage on the British cartographic ship H.M.S. *Beagle* changed the face of modern science and our understanding of human existence. After stops along the coast of South America, the *Beagle* explored the Galápagos Islands, left, an isolated volcanic archipelago straddling the equator. It was there that Darwin noticed that each island was home to species of finches whose beaks differed in size and structure from those on other islands. From this observation Darwin later extrapolated his theory of natural selection, the evolutionary process by which organisms with superior adaptive characteristics survive and pass on those qualities.

The discovery's troubling conclusion: humans could thus be an accident of natural selection, not a direct product of God. "The subject haunted me," Darwin later wrote. (In fact, his worries about how much his theory would shake society's underpinnings exacerbated the ongoing illnesses he suffered.)

More than 150 years after *On the Origin of Species* was published, backers of creationism still fight to keep evolution out of schools. Yet Darwinism is one of the most successful scientific theories ever promulgated. Hardly any element of humanity—not capitalism, not gender relations, certainly not biology—can be fully understood without its help. Dead since 1882, Darwin still challenges our world.

Long-Distance Operator: 1847-1922

Alexander G. Bell

MARCH 1876: IN THE ATTIC OF A Boston boardinghouse, two young scientists were working at top speed. One was a Scottish-born teacher of the deaf, Alexander Graham Bell; the other was an American, Thomas A. Watson. Following Bell's instructions Watson had constructed the first crude telephone, but the results were disappointing. Sounds came over the wire, but no intelligible words.

The men were constructing a new transmitter, in which a diaphragm of thin cow's membrane was attached to a wire carrying an electric current, which in turn was dipped in diluted sulfuric acid. To test the device, they installed a line connecting the front and back rooms. Watson went to the front room, took up his post at the receiver. In his excitement, Bell in the back room drenched his clothes with acid spilled from a battery. He called into the transmitter, "Mr. Watson, come here; I want you." Trembling with jubilation, Watson rushed to the back room crying, "I heard you! I heard you!" At that point Bell forgot all about his ruined clothing.

That scene is one of science's great eureka moments. Yet its very fame, and the impact and ubiquity of the telephone, has overshadowed the breadth and depth of the career of Bell, one of science's great modern Renaissance men. Only 29 when he uttered his famous plea to Watson, Bell went on to explore a host of new frontiers and perfect a dazzling array of new devices, including the first metal detector and an improved phonograph, the graphophone. (Both Bell's mother and his wife were deaf, and he was a lifelong student of hearing and acoustics.)

Bell was a pioneer of magnetic recording, hydrofoil watercraft and airplane design. He helped fund the start-up of *Science* magazine and helped found the National Geographic Society, becoming its second president. He even explored genetics at his estate in Nova Scotia, working for 30 years to breed female sheep with more nipples than the standard two, thus increasing their fecundity. He was, after all, well versed in the power of fecundity.

Patenting Progress: 1847-1931

MUCH OF THE WORLD WE LIVE in today is a legacy of Thomas Alva Edison and of his devotion to science and innovation. He not only invented the first commercial electric light bulb but also established the first investor-owned electric utility, in 1882, on Pearl Street in New York City. His phonograph, invented in 1877, launched a global recorded-music industry that is worth nearly $150 billion today. But more than a simple series of inventions, Edison's most lasting contribution might be the system of industrial innovation he helped pioneer.

Edison's true genius lay in his ability to bring mass brainpower to the process of invention. The laboratory and workshop he established in Menlo Park, N.J., in 1876—his "invention factory"—put him at the center of a critical mass of assistants with backgrounds in multiple areas of science, engineering and skilled labor. It was essentially America's first industrial R&D facility, the forerunner of a modern-day geeks-in-a-garage skunkworks.

Edison patented 1,093 mechanisms and processes, including a stock ticker, a mimeograph, a microphone, a mechanical vote recorder and a battery for an electric car. He came up with the crucial devices that gave birth to three enduring industries: electrical power, recorded music and motion pictures. Yet he was an odd sort of hero: a millionaire who often slept in a closet at the lab with his clothes on; a picturesque swearer who hired assistants whom George Bernard Shaw called "sensitive, cheerful and profane; liars, braggarts and hustlers"; a would-be tycoon so bullheaded that he could give little credit to the ideas of others; a businessman so inept that he lost control of the hugely profitable companies he founded. "Anything that won't sell, I don't want to invent," he said. "Its sale is proof of utility, and utility is success." By his own yardstick, he was wildly successful.

Visionary of Computing: 1791-1871

AS LONG AS MATHEMATICS HAS existed, computers have existed. The trouble with those computers was that before Charles Babbage, they were human. In the 19th century, serious number-crunching involved huge published tables of logarithms, which were computed by hand, and by head, with great effort and expense and an inevitable element of fallibility. When the Age of Steam arrived, and with it the Industrial Revolution, it became possible to produce in bulk, with machines, things that were previously handmade. But it took an extraordinary mind to realize that a machine could be used to produce not just tangible objects but also abstract calculations. That mind belonged to Babbage.

Born in England in 1791, Babbage had a precocious interest in mathematics, which he would eventually apply to a bogglingly diverse array of subjects, including life insurance, the postal service, train schedules and the care of livestock, as well as a table enumerating the 464 different ways that plate-glass windows can get broken. But we remember him for the Difference Engine, and later the Analytical Engine. They were, as he put it, his attempts to "throw the powers of thought into wheel-work."

Beginning in 1823 Babbage's work was funded by the British government, to which he promised "logarithmic tables as cheap as potatoes." What he gave them was an extraordinary machine—or part of one, anyway. The Difference Engine was a thing of cogs and gears and dials and rotors, manufactured in brass and pewter at a level of precision never previously achieved. It took Babbage 10 years, and thousands of pounds, to produce a partial working prototype. Eventually he ran out of funds, and the machine was never completed.

But Babbage didn't stop dreaming. By 1835 he had conceived of an Analytical Engine that could handle variables and store up to a thousand numbers in memory. It would accept input in the form of punch cards, the way industrial looms did, and it would be, in a limited way, programmable. It was never fully built—its one completed component is shown above—but Babbage's imaginary engine would have been the first to meet modern definitions of what a computer is.

Babbage didn't live to see his thoughts become wheel-work, let alone silicon, but he was the first to threaten biology's monopoly on intelligence. In 1842 Tennyson penned the lines "Every minute dies a man/ Every minute one is born." Babbage wrote a letter to Tennyson correcting him on his math, and suggested a more statistically accurate alternative: "Every moment dies a man/ And one and a 16th is born." He had crunched the numbers.

—By Lev Grossman

Louis Pasteur

Pioneer of Healing: 1822-95

THE FRENCH SCIENTIST AND physician Louis Pasteur was among the pioneers who helped midwife modern medical practice, often working with gifted collaborators to overturn centuries of received but errant wisdom. One of a number of scientists who developed germ theory, he laid the groundwork for British physician Joseph Lister, who established healthy practices of antisepsis for medical practitioners, saving thousands of lives. Pasteur's investigation of bacteria and other organisms that are essential to our health make him one of the founders of the field of microbiology. It was Pasteur who was foremost in developing the theory of immunity and in pioneering its invaluable application, vaccination, while his work with fermentation resulted in the lifesaving procedure that bears his name, the pasteurization of liquids.

Pasteur finally, and firmly, overturned the ancient, spurious theory of spontaneous generation with his new understanding of bacteria and other microbes. His exploration of the workings of the body also led him into chemistry, where he left his mark in the study of crystals and their molecular structure. And, like his American near contemporary, Thomas Edison, Pasteur helped develop modern methods of group research, founding the Pasteur Institute to continue his studies of disease and its prevention.

Lumière Brothers

Film's First Family
Auguste, 1862-1954
Louis, 1864-1948

AS PHOTOGRAPHY CAPTIVATED the world, many inventors sought to create moving pictures: a series of photographs, taken in fast sequence, that could capture realistic movement on film. By the 1890s, several such systems had been developed, notably the kinetoscope process created by Thomas Edison and his employee William Dickson.

The kinetoscope included many of the hallmarks of later movie technology, including film perforated on the sides that was ratcheted past a high-speed shutter. But when it came to watching the resulting films, Edison and Dickson thought inside the box: kinetoscope images were viewed at a small size, inside a small booth, by one person at a time. It was a pair of French brothers, Auguste and Louis Lumière, who came up with the breakthrough notion of using a powerful light source to project the moving images onto a screen large enough to be viewed by many people at once, creating the communal feeling of theater in a powerful new medium they called *cinéma*.

The Lumière brothers showed their first moving pictures on Dec. 28, 1895, to 33 astonished Parisians; within days, lines outside the *Cinématographe Lumière* stretched for a quarter of a mile. But when the "movies" became an art form, the brothers moved on. "I was not an artist," said Louis. Perhaps. Yet the Lumières' creation became an art form that has moved humans everywhere.

Magellan of the Mind: 1856-1939

THERE ARE NO NEUTRALS IN THE Freud wars: admiration, even downright adulation, on one side; skepticism, even downright disdain, on the other. But on one thing the contending parties agree: Sigmund Freud, more than any other explorer of the psyche, shaped the mind of the modern age. Embittered confrontations have dogged the footsteps of the Moravian-born Jew since he developed the cluster of theories he would give the name of psychoanalysis. His fundamental idea—that all humans are endowed with an unconscious in which potent sexual and aggressive drives, and defenses against them, struggle for supremacy, as it were, behind a person's back—has struck many as a romantic, scientifically unprovable notion. His contention that the catalog of neurotic ailments to which humans are susceptible is nearly always the work of sexual maladjustment, and that erotic desire starts not in puberty but in infancy, seemed to respectable folk nothing less than obscene. His dramatic evocation of a universal Oedipus complex seems more like a literary conceit than a thesis worthy of a scientifically minded psychologist.

As a brilliant student pursuing medical research in Vienna, Freud came to the conclusion that the most intriguing mysteries lay concealed in the complex operations of the mind. By the early 1890s, he was specializing in "neurasthenics" (mainly severe hysterics); they taught him much, including the art of patient listening. The book that made his reputation, *The Interpretation of Dreams* (1899), is an indefinable masterpiece: part dream analysis, part autobiography, part theory of the mind, part history of contemporary Vienna. In his best-known essay, "Civilization and Its Discontents" (1930), he noted that the human animal, with its insatiable needs, must always remain an enemy to organized society, which exists largely to tamp down sexual and aggressive desires. At best, civilized living is a compromise between wishes and repression—not a comfortable doctrine. It ensures that Freud, taken straight, will never become truly popular, even if today we all speak Freud.

—By Peter Gay

Sigmund Freud

Albert Einstein

Relativity's Revelator: 1879-1955

HE WAS THE GREATEST MIND AND paramount icon of our age, the kindly, absentminded professor whose wild halo of hair, piercing eyes, engaging humanity and extraordinary brilliance made his face a symbol and his name a synonym for genius: Albert Einstein.

During his spare time as a young technical officer in a Swiss patent office in 1905, the young German produced three papers that changed science forever. The first described how light could behave not only like a wave but also like a stream of particles, called quanta or photons. This wave-particle duality became the foundation of what is known as quantum physics. It also provided theoretical under-pinnings for such 20th century advances as television, lasers and semiconductors. The second paper confirmed the existence of molecules and atoms by statistically showing how their random collisions explained the jerky motion of tiny particles in water.

But it was his third paper that truly up-ended the universe. It was based, like much of Einstein's work, on a thought experiment: no matter how fast one is moving toward or away from a source of light, the speed of that light beam will appear the same, a constant 186,000 miles per second. But space and time will appear relative. The special theory of relativity went on to show that energy and matter were merely different faces of the same thing, their relationship defined by the most famous equation in physics: energy equals mass multiplied by the speed of light squared, $E=mc^2$. Although not exactly a recipe for an atom bomb, the theory explained why one was possible.

In 1916 Einstein published his general theory of relativity, which posited gravity as a warping of space-time. It took three years for astronomers to prove the theory by showing how the

sun's gravity shifted light coming from a star. The results were announced at a meeting of the Royal Society in London presided over by J.J. Thomson, who in 1897 had discovered the electron. After glancing up at a grand portrait of Sir Isaac Newton, Thomas told the assemblage, "Our conceptions of the fabric of the universe must be fundamentally altered."

—By Walter Isaacson

Elemental Visionary: 1867-1934

Marie Curie

MARIE SKLODOWSKA WAS BORN into an intellectual Warsaw family: her father had been a physics professor, her mother principal of a girls' school. Their daughter had to flee to Paris because overbearing Russian officials frowned on her efforts to stimulate interest in the Polish language. While studying at the Sorbonne she lived in a bare garret, ate cheap meals and met a brooding, handsome young physics instructor, Pierre Curie, whom she twitted for expressing astonishment at her command of science, and then married.

Henri Becquerel's accidental discovery of the radioactivity of uranium compounds in 1896 greatly excited the young scientists. They obtained a ton of pitchblende from the Austrian government and began a long series of crushings, leachings, precipitations, crystallizations with rudimentary apparatus. Marie spent hours stirring a cauldron with an iron rod as thick as one of her thin arms. At last they had a thimbleful of a white salt. In it they found first polonium and then radium.

Curie became the first female professor at the Sorbonne and the first female Nobel laureate; together with Pierre, she was awarded half the Nobel Prize in Physics in 1903 for their work in spontaneous radiation (Becquerel was awarded the other half). She became the only person to receive Nobels in two different scientific categories—she also was awarded the prize in chemistry in 1911.

Curie was serene, dignified, dedicated. Albert Einstein is said to have remarked that Curie, "of all celebrated beings, [is] the only one whom fame has not corrupted." She poured her prize money into further research. The payoffs were many and varied, including an unprecedented and unrepeated string of Nobels won by one family: her daughter Irène and her son-in-law Frédéric Joliot-Curie won the Nobel Prize in Chemistry in 1935 for their discovery of artificial radioactivity. The downsides were also great. Marie's work with radioactive elements inflicted serious burns to her arms and hands—and perhaps triggered the aplastic anemia that killed her at age 66.

Masters of Gravity
Wilbur, 1867-1912
Orville, 1871-1948

Wright Brothers

WILBUR AND ORVILLE WRIGHT were two brothers from the heartland of America with a vision as sweeping as the sky and a practicality as down-to-earth as the Wright Cycle Co., the bicycle shop they founded in Dayton, Ohio, in 1892. But while there were many bicycle shops in their America, in only one were wings being built as well as wheels.

The brothers were long fascinated by the idea of flight. The force of their obsession led them to develop, single-handedly, the technologies they needed to pursue their dream. When standard aeronautical data proved unreliable, they built their own wind tunnel to learn how to lift a flying machine into the sky (in the photo on this page, they are test-flying a glider). They were the first to discover that a long, narrow wing shape was the ideal architecture of flight. They figured out how to move the vehicle freely up and down on a cushion of air. They built a forward elevator to control the pitch of their craft and fashioned a pair of twin rudders in back to control its tendency to yaw from side to side. They devised a pulley system that warped the shape of the wings in midflight to turn the plane and to stop it from rolling laterally in the air.

When the Wrights discovered that a lightweight gas-powered engine did not exist, they decided to design and build their own. It produced 12 horsepower and weighed only 152 lbs. Result: the powered 1903 *Flyer,* a skeletal flying machine of spruce, ash and muslin, with a wingspan of 40 ft. and an unmanned weight of just over 600 lbs. On Dec. 17, 1903, with Orville at the controls, the *Flyer* lifted off shakily from the sand dunes of Kitty Hawk, N.C., and flew 120 ft.—a distance little more than half the wingspan of a Boeing 747-400. That 12-sec. flight changed the world, lifting humans to new heights of freedom and giving us access to places we had never dreamed of reaching.

—*By Bill Gates*

Henry Ford

Prime Mover: 1863-1947

HE DIDN'T INVENT THE AUTO-mobile, but Henry Ford pretty much invented the modern world, transforming transportation and bringing manufacturing and society along for the ride. As Lee Iacocca, who began his auto career at Ford in the 1940s, wrote in TIME, "The boss was a genius. He was an eccentric. He was no prince in his social attitudes and his politics. But Henry Ford's impact in history is almost unbelievable." In 1905, when Ford's backers insisted that the best way to increase profits was to build a car for the rich, he argued that the workers who built the cars ought to be able to afford one themselves.

Ford's Model T, released in 1908, was elegantly simple—and affordable. "Ford instituted industrial mass production," Iacocca noted, "but what really mattered to him was mass consumption. He figured that if he paid his factory workers a real living wage and produced more cars in less time for less money, everyone would buy them ... it was a virtuous circle, and he was the ringmaster." His vision helped create a middle class in the U.S., one marked by urbanization, rising wages and free time for workers to spend their pay.

Ford helped develop an infrastructure of dealer-franchisers, gas stations and better roads to support his cars. His great strength was the manufacturing process, not invention. The company's assembly line in Highland Park, Mich., humming along in 1914 to churn out a new car every 93 minutes, threw America's Industrial Revolution into overdrive. The same year, Ford doubled his workers' wages, helping more of them buy more cars. His views of race and history are a blot on his legacy—and he let General Motors lap Ford Motor with stronger marketing—but his impact on our world is undeniable.

Joyride *Henry Ford takes a spin in his 1896 runabout in 1946, as he celebrates the 50th anniversary of his first automobile*

Code Crackers
Francis Crick, 1916-2004
James Watson, 1928-

THE 20TH CENTURY'S GREATEST biological breakthrough was announced unceremoniously on Feb. 28, 1953, when British scientist Francis Crick (on right, above) winged into the Eagle Pub in Cambridge, England, and declared that he and his younger U.S. partner, James Watson, had "found the secret of life."

That morning Watson had sketched out how four chemical bases paired to create a self-copying code at the core of the double-helix-shaped DNA molecule, heredity's master switch. In their more formal one-page paper in the journal *Nature,* they noted the significance of their discovery in a famously understated sentence: "It has not escaped our notice that the specific pairing we have postulated immediately suggests a possible copying mechanism for the genetic material." But they were less restrained when asking Watson's sister to type up the paper for them. "We told her," Watson wrote in his account of their discovery, *The Double Helix,* "that she was participating in perhaps the most famous event in biology since Darwin's book." Another woman played a more significant role: X-ray diffraction images taken by British scientist Rosalind Franklin helped the two men describe the double-helical structure of DNA and spark an ongoing biological revolution.

—*By Walter Isaacson*

Watson & Crick

Back on top *Jobs poses in his trademark uniform at Apple's Cupertino, Calif., campus in 2002*

Digital Visionary: 1955-2011

H E WAS THE HIGH PRIEST OF THE computer age, and as the pancreatic cancer that would kill him at age 56 took its toll, he appeared ever more gaunt and ascetic in his uniform of jeans and black turtleneck at the live introductions of his latest Apple products. There was always something of the monkish seeker about Steve Jobs, from his days as a part-time student at Reed College in Oregon, through his *Wanderjahr* in Asia to his pursuit of perfection in the dazzling products he and his colleagues created.

His business career started where all the best Silicon Valley stories begin: with two pals fiddling with computers in a garage. While IBM and other large firms were creating huge mainframe machines, Jobs and his software-genius partner, Steve Wozniak, cooked up the first small personal computer, the Apple II. Then, thanks to a visit to Xerox's local research lab, Jobs got a glimpse of the future: a computer with a graphical design interface, operated by a mouse. Inspired, he drove his Apple team to create a giant stride forward in digital design, the Macintosh computer. Debuting

in 1984, it swept the world, and by age 25, Jobs's net worth was $100 million. But he was a tough, abrasive, pushy manager, and after his failings as an executive led to his ouster from his own company, Jobs entered a period of exile in which he founded a new computer company, NeXT, and ran Pixar, an innovative studio that revolutionized film animation with its 1995 computer-generated hit, *Toy Story*.

By 1997 Apple was on the skids, a victim of executives who lacked Jobs' vision. He returned to his former company, retooled it—and commenced the greatest comeback in business history, introducing a clutch of breakthrough products that created a new digital landscape: the iPod, the iTunes store, the iPhone, the iPad. Apple's retail outlets became the highest-grossing stores in the world, and as of 2012, Apple was the world's most valuable company.

Jobs was a visionary whose great genius was for design: he pushed and pushed to make the interface between computers and people elegant, simple and delightful. He always claimed his goal was to create products that were "insanely great." Mission accomplished.

Steve Jobs

Other Exceptional Explorers

Two travelers and a scientist pursued new frontiers

Leif Eriksson
c. 975-1020

When Leif Eriksson was born, the swift ships of his fellow Norsemen were the most advanced sailing vessels on the planet. His father Erik the Red was a seaman who sailed west from Scandinavia and founded a Norse settlement in today's Iceland. After a few years, Erik moved on, apparently after killing a neighbor, and founded around A.D. 985 the first Norse foothold in Greenland.

It was Erik's son Leif who sailed even farther west, landing sometime around the year 1000 in a place he called Vinland. There he constructed a settlement that endured for several years before its inhabitants returned to Scandinavia, for reasons unknown. Leif's feat faded from memory until the 1960s, when the ruins of Norse buildings in today's Newfoundland were discovered. It was not until Columbus' voyage almost 500 years later that the New World was firmly "discovered."

Marco Polo
c. 1254-1324

The Travels of Marco Polo is one of the most influential books in history. Probably dictated in 1298, it is described by China scholar Jonathan Spence as "a combination of verifiable fact, random information posing as statistics, exaggeration, make-believe ... and a certain amount of outright fabrication." Yet however imprecise, the 14th century version of *On the Road* was treated as news by captivated Europeans, tantalizing them with the notion of an advanced, yet highly exotic, civilization in China.

Marco Polo, a Venetian merchant, was intrigued by his father's and uncle's passages through Central Asia and undertook with them a 24-year journey to the East, during which he met Genghis Khan's grandson and ruler of China, Kublai Khan. Opening Europe's eyes to the wonders of a wider world, *Travels* helped kick-start the Age of Discovery, which would take Europe into a fateful era of exploration and colonization of other nations.

MARCVS POLVS

Guglielmo Marconi
1874-1937

In the late 19th century, Scottish physicist James Clerk Maxwell and German physicist Heinrich Hertz discovered the existence of radio waves, a form of electromagnetic radiation. Italy's Guglielmo Marconi believed these waves could be harnessed to send messages.

A clutch of other inventors also pursued this goal. But it was Marconi who, by the early 1900s, had filed or bought key patents in radio technology and was sending wireless messages through the air. In 1901 he demonstrated the power of the new medium by sending the first radio message, in Morse code, across the Atlantic Ocean, from Cornwall in Britain to Newfoundland in Canada.

Radio technology would lead to TV technology, and Marconi's wireless, which he saw as an updated telegraph, was further transformed in the 1920s when it was repurposed to broadcast news and entertainment to large audiences. Radio thus became the first electronic mass medium.

Leaders of the

QUOTATIONS FROM
CHAIRMAN
MAO TSE-TUNG

敬祝毛主席万寿

People

Creatures of the political world, they led armies, built nations, forged empires, challenged authority, fought for freedom, oppressed—and liberated—the masses. They are the powerful.

From left: Augustus Caesar, Roman coin; George Washington, by Currier & Ives; Cleopatra VII, Egyptian statue; Mao Zedong's Little Red Book

Great Emancipator: c. 1520-1400 B.C.

Moses

HE WAS MARKED BY HIS IMPER-fections. He stammered. He oftentimes hated the very people he led. Almost as frequently, he was at odds with the God who sent him on his mission—and thus, in the end, the God who worked wonders through him kept Moses from the wonder that was his life's longing, the Promised Land. There have been few lives more memorable. He was raised among the privileged princes of Egypt, only to throw in his lot with slaves. He would lead his oppressed people safely through a valley of watery death that had been cleaved into the sea. A pillar of smoke guided them by day, a pillar of fire by night. And on the heights of Mount Sinai, above a world filled with idols, Moses walked into the terrifying presence of the divine and declared that God is One.

Moses is a universal symbol of liberation,

God Parted the Clouds, from *The Story of the Exodus,* by Marc Chagall, 1965-68

law and leadership, sculpted by Michelangelo, painted by Rembrandt, eulogized by Elie Wiesel as "the most solitary and most powerful hero in biblical history ... After him, nothing else was the same again."

He was an irresistible personality, a man both weak and strong, a prophet both happily and unhappily caught up in the whirlwind of God. The venerated images rush to mind: the burning bush, the ten plagues and the Ten Commandments, the dread night of Passover, the dry rock bursting with water, manna from heaven, the golden calf. He was a mighty man of the spirit, but he was also one of history's great rebels, leading his flock out of slavery and into a bright new world of law, justice and devotion to the Lord: the Promised Land. As one who spoke truth to power and risked his life to bring justice to his world, he led the way for Luther, Gandhi, King and Mandela.

Pericles

Voice of Democracy
C. 495-429 B.C.

PERICLES WAS THE FIRST CITIZEN of ancient Athens. As expander of its empire, patron of its culture and embodiment of its spirit, he led Classical Greece's foremost city-state during its foremost age. Though nobly born, he emerged in his 30s as an advocate for the common people, urging their wider participation in civic life. After helping ostracize his political foe, Cimon, Pericles became Athens' first citizen in 461 B.C. and was its leader for the next 30 years.

A capable general, Pericles helped expand the Athenian empire, the Delian League, in a series of wars against barbarians and other Greek city-states. As a statesman, he fostered inclusive democratic reforms for Athens' citizens (if not for the slaves who maintained the city's glory). He envisioned, funded and supervised the building of the Parthenon and other structures on the Acropolis, earning a place as one of history's greatest builders.

Near the end of his career, Pericles led Athens into the First Peloponnesian War with Sparta, an avoidable conflict that shook his standing with the people of the city. Even so, he delivered a memorable funeral oration for Athens' war dead in 431 B.C., powerfully articulating many of the ideals of Western democracy. Two years later, this early advocate for government of, by and for the people died amid an epidemic in Greece.

Ashoka the Great

Wise Emperor: 304-232 B.C.

HE IS KNOWN TO INDIANS AS "THE Emperor of Emperors," and his era is recalled as a golden age of civility, compassion and culture. Yet the long reign of Ashoka the Great, third ruler of Asia's Maurya dynasty, began amid bloodshed and strife. Ashoka's grandfather Chandragupta Maurya had founded the Maurya Empire, the first to unite the Indian subcontinent and its neighbors, from Bengal in the east to Afghanistan in the west, and from Kashmir and Nepal in the north to the Deccan Plateau in the south. The young Ashoka was a ruthless warrior who won the throne by the sword after disposing of a passel of half-brothers. But after he defeated the kingdom of Kalinga in eastern India at the cost of 100,000 enemy lives, he is said to have recoiled at the bloodshed and undergone a religious conversion, pledging his life to Buddha and his principles of nonviolence.

In the years that followed, Ashoka helped convert large swaths of India and Southeast Asia to Buddhism, although only a small minority of Indians follow Buddhism today. He erected obelisks across his empire to proclaim his just laws; dozens of them still stand today. He built roads and irrigation systems, universities, stupas and monasteries. Above all, he built a reputation as one of history's most enlightened and farsighted monarchs.

Alexander in Combat, artist unknown, c. 4th century B.C.

King of Conquest: 356-323 B.C.

WHEN ALEXANDER THE GREAT died—far too soon, at only 32—legend has it that the men assigned to embalm him trembled at their task, afraid that they were touching the body of a god. That would have pleased the young prince of Macedon, who certainly acted like a god. At the age of 16 he crushed a Thracian rebellion and founded a city that he named after himself, the first of many. After the death of his father King Philip II, Alexander, all of 20, conquered Greece, won its allegiance, then went off on a war of revenge against Persia. Thebes rebelled; he razed it to the ground (with remorse). He won the Battle of Issus, ending Asiatic rule in the Mediterranean. He then took Tyre and Egypt and defeated Darius III, leader of the Persian Empire, at Gaugamela in what was the most important battle in antiquity: it made way for the Hellenistic age, which lasted from Alexander's death in 323 B.C. to the time of Augustus, some 20 years before the birth of Jesus. Famously in search of more worlds to conquer, Alexander turned to Central Asia and India, and at his death, his kingdom reached from Illyria on the west to Kashmir on the east, and from Egypt to China. His troops loved him, and he never lost a battle.

He was more than a power-mad conquistador: Alexander's vision of empire was diverse, humanistic, progressive. His father had hired Aristotle to instruct his son, and historians and botanists traveled with his armies. He acted as if he did not merely seek to conquer all creation but also to make sense of it.

Cleopatra

Female Pharaoh: 69-30 B.C.

CLEOPATRA VII WAS THE HINGE between two Caesars: the powerful Pharaoh of ancient Egypt was the lover of Julius Caesar and the enemy of Augustus Caesar. She was the seventh Pharaoh of the Ptolemaic dynasty, Macedonians who took control of Egypt in the Hellenistic era. Rivalry with her brother and co-ruler, Ptolemy, had driven her from the throne when she first met Julius Caesar, who had come to Egypt in pursuit of his enemy, Pompey. Reputedly a great beauty, Cleopatra became Caesar's mistress, and he restored her to the throne. After the two had a child, Caesarion, Cleopatra followed Caesar to Rome and was in the city when he was slain.

After Caesar's death, Cleopatra became the partner and lover of Mark Antony, who had formed a ruling Second Triumvirate with Octavian (the future Augustus Caesar) and Lepidus, Julius Caesar's cavalry commander. But when these three leaders quarreled and civil war broke out, Antony and Cleopatra's forces were defeated twice by Octavian's, in a naval battle at Actium and a land battle at Alexandria. Distraught, the two lovers committed suicide; Cleopatra, legend holds, by snakebite. Octavian rose to become Rome's first Emperor, while Cleopatra's beauty, lust for life, political acuity and dramatic demise made her history's first female superstar.

Empire Builder: 63 B.C.-14 A.D.

AUGUSTUS CAESAR, BORN GAIUS Octavius, led imperial Rome's greatest era. He rose to power amid the long series of civil wars that began when his great-uncle, Julius Caesar, became dictator. Named the heir of the assassinated leader, Octavian began his political career at only 18, forming the Second Triumvirate with Lepidus and Mark Antony. But the three eventually clashed: Lepidus was driven to the sidelines, and after a long series of battles that demonstrated his mastery of politics, public relations and warfare, Octavian finally triumphed over Antony and his ally and lover, Cleopatra, in 31 B.C. Four years later he was firmly established as Rome's primary ruler.

In the four decades that followed, Octavian, now known as Augustus Caesar, completely restructured his city and realm. An Emperor in all but title, he carefully maintained a façade of republicanism, living simply and devoting himself to cultivating the empire's riches rather than his own. The Pax Romana he began was a period of relative internal peace that lasted for almost 200 years, during which the extent of Rome's holdings steadily increased, thanks to capable generals, while its internal operations steadily improved, thanks to policies introduced by Augustus.

As Rome's leader, he reformed the empire's tax code, instituted its uniform legal system and built great roads, aqueducts and public facilities to unite its lands and encourage its commerce. He shrewdly managed relations with the masses and the military, using the army's support to dominate the Senate. He also rebuilt his city, making it the wonder of the world and declaring, "I found Rome built in brick, I leave her clad in marble." Upon his death, a grateful Senate declared him a god.

Master of Rome *A bronze statue of Augustus stands along the city's Via dei Fori Imperiale*

Augustus Caesar

LIKE CONSTANTINOPLE, THE GREAT city he founded, the Roman Emperor Constantine I bestrides cultures, religions and historical epochs. He was the first Emperor to embrace Christianity, and he turned the empire's orientation to the east.

Constantine was born in today's Serbia in a period of Roman decline, the son of Flavius Constantius, a rising general under the Emperor Diocletian. Constantine became a great warrior, earning his stripes on campaigns with Diocletian in Asia and the Middle East. His youth was consumed by struggles in a period when imperial rule was split among four, and sometimes six, contenders. He succeeded his father in ruling vast parts of the western empire, including Britain, Gaul and Spain. The best general of his time, he

Constantine the Great

invaded Italy to challenge his chief rival for power, Maxentius. In the Battle of the Milvian Bridge on the Tiber River in A.D. 312, Constantine prevailed over Maxentius, after receiving a vision that urged him to have his troops wear Christian symbols, even though Christianity was outlawed and its adherents had been cruelly persecuted by Diocletian.

Constantine entered Rome as the strongest of four rulers in a contentious Tetrarchy and spent the next few years consolidating his power and adorning the city. In 313 he and Licinius, a fellow Tetrarch, met in Milan and issued an edict that recognized the legitimacy of Christianity for the first time in imperial history. In the years that followed, Constantine first quarreled, then battled directly with Licinius, whose power base was in the eastern empire. In the year 324, the two fought a mighty civil war. Constantine defeated Licinius in three battles, at last emerging as the empire's sole ruler.

Constantine now sought to unite his vast empire and to integrate its eastern and western realms. Choosing the Greek town of Byzantium, at the junction of Europe and Asia, as his capital, he poured wealth into the creation of a spectacular new Rome of the East, Constantinople (now Istanbul). Here a proud new empire would flourish, symbolized by the historic basilica the Hagia Sophia, below, whose first version was built by Constantine's son. The Hagia Sophia would witness the rise of the Byzantine Empire and the schism that separated Christianity into two rival sects in 1054 before becoming a mosque when Constantinople fell to conquering Turks in 1453.

The First Four Caliphs, by V. Raineri, 19th century

Umar ibn al-Khattab

Architect of Empire
c. 588-644

SELDOM IN WORLD HISTORY HAS A new social force ignited with more power: following the death of the Prophet Muhammad in A.D. 632, Islam seemed to explode outward from the Arabian Peninsula. Armed with the zeal of new converts, the Prophet's disciples carried his message across Africa, the Middle East and Central Asia. No single man did more to advance Islam's growth than Umar ibn al-Khattab, a Mecca-born, longtime colleague of the Prophet's who became the second Caliph to succeed Muhammad as the leader of Islam.

As Caliph, Umar looked to the east: his armies conquered the great Sassenid Empire in Persia and also took control of two-thirds of the Byzantine Empire. But his genius tended more to administration than warfare: he created the infrastructure that drove Islam's continuing expansion, placed the military firmly under civilian control, established a fair and just system of laws, fostered scholarship and the arts and treated Christians and Jews with respect. Widely admired for his resolve and wisdom, he eschewed luxury and lived simply and humbly. Entrusted with the care of a newborn religion, he led it into maturity.

Europe's Father: circa 742-814

BORN AT A TIME WHEN AN AVER-age man reached 5 ft. 5 in. (165 cm) in height, he topped out at 6 ft. 3 in. (192 cm). His impact matched his size: in an age when power flowed from the mace and the sword, he was the era's strongest warlord—and also became its most farsighted visionary, its most capable politician, its most effective patron of the arts. No wonder Charles, King of the Franks, is known to history as Charles the Great, Carolus Magnus or Charlemagne.

Sired to rule, Charles cast his lot with the papacy after inheriting the Frankish throne from his father in A.D. 768. He protected Pope Adrian I by invading Italy and defeating the Lombards, then moved west to follow in the footsteps of his grandfather Charles Martel and fight the Moorish rulers in Spain. But there Charles met his match; he was defeated by a Basque army at the Battle of Ronces-valles in A.D. 778. Undeterred, he continued his path of conquest, bringing Corsica and Sardinia under Frankish control. Finally he returned to northern Europe to battle pagan Saxons, beating them in a long campaign and forcing them to convert to Christianity.

Most at home on horseback with his celebrated sword Joyeuse in his hand, Charles battled for more than three decades to bring a wide swath of Europe under his sway: he conquered Bavaria; fought Croats and Slavs in southeast Europe; battled Avars, an invading Asian horde, in Hungary. By A.D. 800 he had united almost all Europe under his control, and Pope Leo III crowned him Holy Roman Emperor in St. Peter's Basilica in Rome.

An enlightened ruler who celebrated learning and scholarship, Charles introduced a new monetary system into his Eurozone 1.0, reformed education and fostered the Carolingian Renaissance, in which Western artists forcefully broke away from Byzantine influence. Agreeing with Charlemagne's contemporaries, in 2004 Pope John Paul II called him *Pater Europae:* the Father of Europe.

Charlemagne

Roland Bidding Farewell to Charlemagne, Grandes Chroniques de France, 14th century

Saladin, by Cristofano dell'Altissimo, 16th century

Saladin

Clement Commander: c. 1138-93

WHEN SALAH AL-DIN YUSUF ibn Ayyub was born in 1138 to a family of Kurdish adventurers in the (now Iraqi) town of Tikrit, Islam was a confusion of squabbling warlords living under a Christian shadow. A generation before, the European knights of the First Crusade had conquered Jerusalem, massacred its Muslim and Jewish inhabitants and created four militarily aggressive states in the Holy Land. Expelling the hated occupiers would require Muslims to work together, but amid treacherous regional crosscurrents, such a united front seemed unlikely.

The death, in 1169, of Shirkuh, the de facto leader of Egypt, allowed the rise of his nephew, Saladin. A seasoned warrior despite his small stature and frailty, Saladin still had a tough hand to play. He was a Kurd (even then a drawback in Middle Eastern politics), and he was from Syria, a Sunni state, trying to rule Egypt, a Shi'ite realm. But in a masterly 17-year campaign, he employed diplomacy, the sword and great good fortune to become lord of Egypt, Syria and much of Mesopotamia.

Now he moved against the Christians. At Hattin, within sight of the Golan Heights, Saladin's pan-Islamic force of 12,000 cavalry overwhelmed a Christian army on July 4, 1187; three months later, the Muslims recaptured Jerusalem. In stark contrast to the Crusaders' bloody conquest, Saladin's warriors neither murdered nor looted. "Christians everywhere will remember the kindness we have bestowed upon them," he said.

And they did. Saladin's humane application of justice to both war and governance influenced Arab rulers for centuries. His tolerance was exemplary; he even allowed Christian pilgrims to visit Jerusalem after its fall. The great Jewish sage Maimonides was his physician. Saladin's reputation for justice and wisdom was such that Dante a century later placed him in "the paradise of the non-Christian Just."

Mighty Mongol *A silk painting of the Khan in his 6os*

Genghis Khan

King of Warlords: c. 1167-1227

HIS FATHER WAS POISONED BY enemies and his widowed mother was chased away from their Mongol tribe with her brood, including her eldest, 9-year-old Temujin. The outcasts ate field mice even as they fought off horse thieves, guarding precious nomad property. Bitterness cultivated a heart of iron in the boy; out of the shadows, he created a nation and the most disciplined fighting force on the planet. Temujin escaped the wild by making a good marriage, then plied diplomacy and a ruthless militancy to win fiercely loyal followers, using death as discipline and looting as reward. Conquered peoples were divided among the armies, swelling the ranks of soldiers, and the technology of enslaved cultures was absorbed like more booty: the catapults developed in Central Asia were deployed against China's stout walls; the explosive bombs pioneered in China were used in Mesopotamia and Europe.

In 1206, the Mongols acclaimed Temujin as Genghis Khan, the "Oceanic Ruler." In the next two decades he conquered a huge empire as he rolled across Eurasia, amassing kingdoms as loot and nations as slaves. The legacy of Genghis Khan is as terrifying as genocide and as dreadful as the Black Death, which followed his horsemen to Europe. But this is the paradox: his legacy is also as seductive as Coleridge's Xanadu and as momentous to history as the discovery of America.

—*By Howard Chua-Eoan*

Saintly Warrior: c. 1412-31

THE 17-YEAR-OLD FRENCH PEAS-
ant girl had a dream—in fact she
had many dreams, visions in which
Christian saints would come to
her, urging her to take up the fight against
the English, who occupied much of northern
France at the time. Improbably, Joan made
her way to the court of Charles, the cowed
French dauphin, or prince, whom many
believed illegitimate. The impassioned teen,
afire with her sacred mission, so impressed

the royals with her holy cause that she was
given armor and troops to command.

Joan, who often dressed in men's attire,
proved her mettle at Orléans, leading an
assault by some 10,000 French troops that
lifted the English siege of the city. A pivotal
victory, it spurred other quick successes and
turned the tide against the English invaders.
On July 17, 1429, Charles was crowned King in
Reims, as urged by Joan. A year later, Joan was
captured by the forces of England's French

Joan of Arc Led to the Stake, by Isidore Patrois, 1867

allies; she was burned to death in May, 1431, in a public square on grounds of heresy and witchcraft. King Charles VII, whose crown had been secured in part by Joan's heroics, did little to try to save her. But on July 17, 1453, Charles' armies ended English rule in France. Economic historians say the railroads made France a nation. Perhaps. But Joan made the people of France want to be a nation.

History and popular legend long ago redeemed Joan; she was canonized in 1920 by the Vatican. She has been painted by Rubens, Rouault and Ingres; she has been portrayed by Sarah Bernhardt, Ingrid Bergman and Jean Seberg; she has been brought to life by writers from Mark Twain to George Bernard Shaw. Although her divine prompting makes Joan a great figure of the spirit, we have placed her among history's warriors and rebels: she fought not only against English rule but also to win a place for women in a medieval society dominated by men.

Isabella of Castile,
by Juan de Flandes, c. 1500

Unifier of Spain: 1451-1504

SHE WAS BORN WHEN THE IBE-rian Peninsula was a patchwork quilt of rival religions, cultures, rulers and fiefs. But by the end of her reign, Queen Isabella I had stabilized and unified Spain and had placed it on a path to becoming what historian J.H. Plumb called "the greatest empire since antiquity." Thanks to Isabella and her husband Ferdinand II of Aragon, much of Europe and most of the New World would become Spain's domain, making the 16th century the Spanish Century.

Few historic couples are spoken of in one breath as much as Isabella and Ferdinand—a testament to the aura surrounding Isabella at a time when most Queens slunk to the margins of history. By many accounts, she was physically unprepossessing but admired for her chastity, piety and prudence. And her record speaks for itself: under her watch, Spain drove out the last Muslim kingdoms on the Iberian Peninsula, cowed Portugal and launched Christopher Columbus to the New World. The galleons of gold and silver that streamed back to Spain in the decades to come were all due to her foresight.

Yet Spain's ascendance on the world stage came at a high cost. Its empire in the New World was built on the bloody conquest of powerful indigenous societies, while the nation's unification involved the expulsion of Jews and Muslims, ending the long, rich period of *convivencia,* when Muslims, Jews and Catholics built a tolerant and enlightened civilization in a Spain dominated by Islam. Imperial Spain also bred the absolutist religious intolerance of the Inquisition. Isabella's legacy may be as diverse as the land she inherited, yet she stands as one of history's great nation builders and visionaries of empire.

Callous Conquistador: 1485-1547

Hernan Cortés

SPAIN'S CONQUEST OF THE AZTEC Empire in Mexico was led by a determined, ruthless man who sought renown, gold and converts to Christianity. Growing up in provincial Medellín in the first years after Columbus sailed to the New World, Hernan Cortés dreamed of glory and ventured to the Americas, arriving at age 19, where he took part in the conquest of Cuba and rose to become an important colonial official.

As Spain sought to expand its foothold in the Americas, Cortés was commissioned to lead one of a series of expeditions against the indigenous peoples of Mexico—and when his patron, Cuba's Governor Diego Velázquez de Cuéllar, reneged on his support, Cortés mutinied and sailed west. Arriving on the Yucatán Peninsula in 1519, he demonstrated his mettle by deliberately scuttling his armada of some 11 ships—a powerful demonstration to his 600 troops that they were now isolated, united and firmly committed to the path of conquest.

The events that followed compose one of history's most unusual—and horrifying—stories of cultural collision. Relying on his native mistress, La Malinche; on the gullibility of the Aztec leader, Montezuma, who may have believed the Spaniard was a god; and on his full-throttle capacity for deceit and cruelty, Cortés and his heavily outnumbered troops managed to unseat Montezuma and take control of his realm. In the following years, Cortés ruthlessly suppressed the indigenous culture of Mexico, aided by European smallpox and other diseases against which the natives had no resistance. And he was among those who introduced African slaves to the New World as an unpaid labor force. Cortés wrote his name on history's wall—in blood.

Face to face *Cortés and La Malinche meet Montezuma in this scene from the illustrated* Codex Tlaxcala, *a Spanish history of the conquest*

Sultan Suleiman, School of Titian, c. 1530

Suleiman the Magnificent

Triumphant Turk: 1494-1566

FOR A FEW WILD WEEKS IN THE summer of 1529, it seemed to be the end of Europe. The ruler Christians called the Unspeakable Turk, Sultan Suleiman, had first smashed the Hungarian capital of Buda; then the invader thundered on, 170 incredible miles (274 km) in one week, to the gates of Vienna. In an instant, faced with a powerful Muslim ruler who commanded a potent army, Europe broke off its feuds. France and the Holy Roman Empire patched up a quick truce; even the Pope and Martin Luther buried the ecclesiastical mace for the time being. Twenty days later, the wily Turk cashed in his chips without a fight, packed up his plunder and poled off down the Danube.

But the career of Sultan Suleiman, 10th and greatest ruler of the Ottoman Turks, had just begun. Suleiman captured vast quadrants of the Middle East and North Africa, all the way to Algeria, for his empire. Indeed, by the time of the great raid on Austria, Suleiman had begun to suspect that he had ridden as far as

he could on the road of conquest, and that it was time to squat on the carpet of diplomacy and consolidate the great adventure into a great state. Accordingly, he struck alliances with France and Venice, reorganized his empire's legal code, expanded its educational system, opened its borders to European immigration and announced the *Pax Turcica*.

The *Pax* was ably defended by a small, deadly force of Janissaries (most of them Christian children, adopted by the state and trained in fanatical devotion to the Sultan) and by Suleiman's new Turkish fleet. Under a pair of his swashbuckling corsairs, the Mediterranean was swept clean, for more than a century, of European fleets. The Sultan showed mercy to his enemies, and he was remarkably faithful to his wife, whom he married, against tradition, out of his harem. A goldsmith and poet, he was also a patron of the arts who presided over a period of lively renascence in Turkish culture. He was, it seems, a quite speakable fellow after all.

Martin Luther as an Augustinian Monk,
by Lucas Cranach the Elder, c. 1523

Martin Luther

Religious Rebel: 1483-1546

IN THE 16TH CENTURY, IF THOSE IN power disagreed with your writing, they usually burned it. If you kept issuing the same document, they usually burned you. Martin Luther, brave and cantankerous soul, kept writing, turning out thousands of pages of crusading sermons, fulminating pamphlets—even many hymns—during his 62 years. He wrote so much, in fact, that he is credited with helping shape the modern German language.

Some of Luther's writings were the doubtful, occasionally anti-Semitic musings of a depressed ex-monk. ("However irreproachably I lived as a monk, I felt myself in the presence of God to be a sinner with a most unquiet conscience," he recalled late in life.) But his doubts led him to question much established wisdom. His *Ninety-Five Theses* (1517) were a potent criticism of papal excess that sparked scores of religious movements known collectively as Protestantism and led to a reformed Roman Catholic Church.

In embracing a view that "faith alone"—not works and certainly not papal indulgences—could bring salvation, Luther propelled the ordinary individual to the heart of religion, urging each of us to think about our own status before God. While his theological views are significant, his achievements as a reformer place him among history's greatest rebels.

Majestic Mughal: 1542-1605

HIS NAME MEANS, LITERALLY, "Great the Great." But if ever a leader merited a tautology, it was India's third Mughal ruler. Under Akbar, a fragile collection of fiefs around Delhi grew into the great Mughal Empire, a diverse kingdom that sprawled across northern India. A canny warlord, Akbar outmaneuvered local Hindu rulers, piling up conquests over a span of two decades to create one of the early modern world's wealthiest states. Below, he rides an elephant into battle in a 17th century miniature.

For Akbar, conquest was a means to an end rather than an end in itself. While Christians staggered haltingly toward achieving what we now know as the Renaissance, Akbar fostered a flourishing of India's arts, sponsoring artisans, poets, engineers and philosophers to create one of the most culturally rich periods in the history of the subcontinent.

While a Muslim, Akbar was spiritually curious and hosted religious scholars, from Hindu gurus to Jesuits, at his vast, diverse court. In his capital city of Fatehpur Sikri, which he built according to astronomical coordinates, he championed a melding of Hinduism and Islam known as the Din-i-Ilahi, or the "Divine Faith." While the creed has not survived, the ethos of pluralism and tolerance that defined Akbar's age underlies the values of the modern republic of India.

Akbar the Great

Queen Elizabeth I

Princess Elizabeth, by Guillaume Scrots, c. 1546

Queen Elizabeth I in Coronation Robes, artist unknown, 1559

Renaissance Royal: 1533-1603

FIRST FEMINIST. FIRST SPINMEIS-
ter. Megawatt celeb. So might our
age judge her. To 16th century England, Elizabeth embodied the original feminine mystique: goddess Gloriana; the
Virgin Queen; and finally and enduringly,
Good Queen Bess. Hers was a prodigious
political success story built on the power of
personality: the Queen as star—a woman so
strong, a politician so skillful, a monarch so
magnetic that she impressed herself indel-
ibly on the minds of her people and reshaped
the fate of England. She brought her country
safely through the Reformation, inspired a

cultural Renaissance and united a tiny, frag-
mented island into a nation of global reach.

Desiring a son, Elizabeth's father Henry
VIII divorced his first wife and broke with
the Roman Catholic Church to marry Anne
Boleyn. When Anne gave birth to a girl, he
ordered his wife beheaded and the child
princess declared a bastard. Elizabeth grew
up in loneliness and danger, learning the
urgency of keeping her balance on England's
quivering political tightrope. She was lucky to
receive a boy's rigorous education, tutored by
distinguished scholars in the classics, history,
philosophy, languages and theology. She was

Queen Elizabeth I, artist unknown, c. 1575-80

Queen Elizabeth I, by John Bettes the Younger, c. 1585-90

serious and quick-witted, but she also loved music, dancing and gaiety.

The bells of London tolled joyously on Nov. 17, 1558, when Elizabeth ascended the throne. She made her coronation the first in a lifetime of scintillant spectacles, visual manifestations of her rule. She restored the country firmly to Protestantism, yet she allowed Catholics freedom of worship, easing the bitter religious strife of Queen Mary's reign. Notoriously parsimonious, she hated war for its wastefulness. Her penny-pinching in 1588 nearly cost England its independence before luck and the skill of her sailors defeated the Spanish armada. Her countrymen gloried in her victory; the battle gave birth to nearly four centuries of patriotic imperialism. She spawned England's empire, chartering seven companies—including the East India—to plunder and colonize in the name of trade.

A larger-than-life royal, Elizabeth came to embody England as few before her. The new spirit emanating from so brilliant a sovereign inspired a flowering of enduring literature, music, drama, poetry. Molding herself into the image of a mighty prince, she made of England a true and mighty nation.

—By Johanna McGeary

Peter the Great

Russia's Renewer: 1672-1725

LIKE CHARLEMAGNE, HE WAS A giant of a man who commanded vision and ambition to match his 6-ft. 7-in. (200 cm) frame. The Czar, who was reputedly strong enough to roll up a silver plate like a parchment scroll, wasn't born Great; he earned his honorific by taking a firm hold on Russia, which he saw as hidebound by stale tradition, and yanking it forcefully into the modern world of the West.

The youngster ascended to rule Russia in 1682 at only 10, sharing his reign with an infirm half-brother; his older half-sister was his regent, literally sitting behind his throne and dictating his policies. It was not until 1696 that he took full control of power in Russia. Bright and determined, he learned from defeat: after his armies were beaten by a smaller Swedish force at Narva in 1700, he remedied his errors, rebuilding, retraining and rearming his entire military, then routing Sweden's King Charles XII at Poltava in 1709.

His victory eventually gave the Russians control of the Baltic states of Estonia and Latvia, and thus a large window to the West.

Determined to build a modern capital on the Baltic, Peter dragooned tens of thousands of soldiers, peasants and prisoners into laboring under such appalling conditions that his creation was said to be built on bones. But in 10 years he laid the foundations for one of the wonders of the world, the parks and canals and esplanades of St. Petersburg.

Like Turkey's Kemal Ataturk in the 20th century, Peter not only updated his nation; he reoriented its vision as well, rejecting Slavic and Byzantine culture for that of Enlightenment Europe. He ordered courtiers and soldiers to trim their long beards and wear European clothes, put Russia on the Julian calendar, even changed the observation of the new year from Sept. 1 to Jan. 1. By his death, Russia had become a great power, and Peter had become Peter the Great.

View of Kazansky Cathedral in St. Petersburg, by Fyodor Alexeyev, c. 1811. Inset: *Peter the Great,* by Jean-Marc Nattier, 1717

George Washington

Cultivator of a Nation: 1732-99

THE LEGEND OF THE MAN IS sheltered these days behind high fences of respect. Were the real Washington on hand today, that might not be the case, and therein may lie a lesson. By our modern measures, George Washington did not read the right books: he relished how-to-do-it texts, with their new ideas on the use of manure, turning soil and animal husbandry. He did not delve very far into art, philosophy or science. Nor did he speak foreign languages (Thomas Jefferson spoke or read five). Washington never traveled to Europe, while Benjamin Franklin, John Adams and Jefferson all spent years there. Aloof and remote, meticulous in his wardrobe, he was not one of the boys, and he was never an accomplished public speaker.

Washington's military achievements are admired for their perseverance rather than their brilliance. The Battle of Trenton might have been as important a conflict as this nation ever won. His victory brought the Revolution back to life: the colonies dared hope again for independence, France began to look with more favor on the American struggle, and Britain began to lose heart. But the battle itself was technically a shambles.

The first President sometimes looked on his 22 years of public service as a kind of prison sentence that took him away from his Virginia estate—Washington accumulated nearly 100,000 acres of land in his last years and was judged one of the wealthiest men in the nation. His favorite recreation was fox hunting, and he was a slaveholder, though, unlike Jefferson, he set his more than 125 slaves free in his will.

George Washington was sensible and wise. He was not the most informed or imaginative of men. But he understood himself and this nation-to-be. His heart and mind were shaped by his family, his land, his community and the small events that touched him every day. He had the tolerance of a landsman, the faith that comes with witnessing the changing seasons year in and year out. Optimism, perseverance, patience and an eager view of the distant horizon have always been a gift of the earth to those who stayed close to it.

Robespierre and Saint-Just Leaving for the Guillotine, by Alfred François Mouillard, 1884. (Robespierre in center with bandaged head)

Maximilien Robespierre

Terror's Tribune: 1758-94

HIS DEVOTED FOLLOWERS CALLED him "the incorruptible." Sadly, he was not; in modern argot, he is the poster boy for revolutionary excess. Maximilien de Robespierre climbed aboard the tiger that was the French Revolution and presided over a period of public terror that foreshadowed those of Hitler, Stalin, Mao and Pol Pot only to find himself devoured by the force he had unleashed.

The unjust and inhumane regimes of France and other Europe nations were badly in need of change as the 18th century waned, but when the oppressed, starving commoners of France finally rose up in 1789 against the nobles and clerics who had refused to share their nation's wealth, their just cause soon devolved into mob rule and a new form of tyranny. Leading the charge was Robespierre, an attorney from Arras and an admirer of the philosophies of Jean-Jacques Rousseau, who stressed each man's innate, natural goodness.

Robespierre did not start the Revolution, but as one biographer observed, he did "drive many people to madness who without him merely would have been fools." He rose with the tide of revolt, first gaining notice as a member of the Estates-General and as a member of the Jacobin Club. A powerful, articulate speaker who lived simply and commanded respect, he was named to the Committee for Public Safety. As the leaders of the Revolution attempted to assert control amid the vacuum of power left by the passing of the monarchy, Robespierre, Georges Danton and other Jacobins put the survival of their cause ahead of all other considerations—including justice.

By 1793, Robespierre was the most powerful figure in the nation, leading a Reign of Terror in which thousands were sent to the guillotine indiscriminately. Soon the leaders themselves fell out: Robespierre sent Danton to the guillotine, and a few months later, he followed him. His life traced a trajectory that is today all too familiar: from reformer to revolutionist to dictator to death. *Sic semper tyrannis.*

Mary Wollstonecraft, by John Keenan, c. 1793

Mary Wollstonecraft

"Hyena in Petticoats": 1759-97

LATE IN 1791, MARY WOLLSTONECRAFT sat down and in six weeks wrote the 300 pages of *A Vindication of the Rights of Women.* Earlier that year, she had broken out of a shell of ladylike anonymity to print a bylined edition of her previously unsigned pamphlet *A Vindication of the Rights of Man,* a loosely reasoned but passionate defense of the French Revolution. Her call for women's rights became an international best seller and exposed the 32-year-old to the baritone wrath of conservatives and liberals alike. She was vilified for arguing that women should be able to achieve financial independence and for suggesting that, given equal education and opportunity, females would be the professional equal of men. British politician Horace Walpole called her a "philosophical serpent" and a "hyena in petticoats."

Had the onetime governess and schoolteacher not stoked herself up to write her call to arms, she would probably have ended up as only a historical footnote: radical editor and translator; wife of philosopher William Godwin; mother of Mary Godwin, future wife of Percy Bysshe Shelley and author of *Frankenstein.* There was a bit of the pathetic patchwork monster about Wollstonecraft herself: a committed romantic, she loved not wisely but too well, attempted suicide and died from septicemia after giving birth to her second child. Her husband's memoir long tainted her reputation, but she is now recognized as a pioneer in the fight for women's rights.

Man on Horseback: 1769-1821

NAPOLEON IS ONE OF THOSE RARE figures in history who arise from nowhere to dominate their age. Early in 1793 he was an untested junior officer in the French army. Eleven years later, in 1804, he was the most commanding figure in a Europe that marched to his martial cadence. That year, the man once seen as the defender of the Revolution summoned Pope Pius VII to Paris to crown him France's new Emperor, left—only to take the diadem from the Pontiff's hand and crown himself.

He was history's classic "man on horseback." Arriving when France was in chaos after the excesses of the Revolution, the military man restored order, acting with decision and dispatch, and became the savior of "the rights of man." As a reward, he was put in command of a French invasion of Italy. The masterly campaign that followed was the first of many triumphs to come. One of history's greatest generals, he reinvented logistics and deployment, speeding up war's pace with fast marches, a brilliant use of artillery and cavalry and unexpected, bold flanking maneuvers. He inspired his soldiers, who loved him.

By 1804 Napoleon controlled much of Europe. At home, he supported science and culture and formulated the Napoleonic Code, enshrining many of the rights articulated in the Revolution. Abroad, campaign followed campaign as a series of coalitions sought to bring him down. As Emperor, his megalomania grew: France took on aspects of a police state, and he embarked on ever more grandiose schemes, stranding his troops in a long campaign on the Iberian Peninsula and waging a foolhardy, failed invasion of Russia in 1812. Defeated at last, he was exiled but managed to escape; he raised another army and had to be beaten yet again. His larger-than-life ride, at full gallop, reminds us that even in a modern age, one person with a strong vision can bend the arc of history in his favor.

The Coronation of Napoleon, by Jacques-Louis David, 1807

Bolívar, by Mexican muralist Fernando Leal, 1931-33

Liberator of Nations: 1783-1830

SOUTH OF THE RIO GRANDE, HE IS known simply as El Libertador—the Liberator. Streets are so commonly emblazoned with that title and statues of Simón Bolívar on horseback are so widely on display in Latin America for good reason: Bolívar played a key role in the independence movements of five modern South American nations. One of them, Bolivia, even named itself after him.

Born into a wealthy Venezuelan family, Bolívar was ejected from his homeland four times before his campaign to overturn the rule of the decaying Spanish Empire was successful. He also helped liberate Colombia, Ecuador and Peru, often collaborating with Argentine revolutionary José de San Martín.

Bolívar's dream of a United States of South America (sans slavery) did not come to pass. Gran Colombia, which included the territories of present-day Colombia, Venezuela, Ecuador and Panama, endured from 1819 to 1831, held together primarily by Bolívar's firm hand: the union dissolved the year after his death in 1830 at only 47. Bolívar's early demise sparked persistent speculation that he had been assassinated; when his body was exhumed in 2010 to test this theory, slight traces of arsenic were found, but not enough to establish that he had been poisoned.

Simón Bolívar

Sitting Bull

Resistance Fighter: c. 1831-90

THE LAKOTA SIOUX CHIEF Sitting Bull is the most famous of a long line of Native Americans who fought bravely to withstand the tide of white European settlers advancing across the continental U.S. His predecessors include Tecumseh, Black Hawk and Osceola; his contemporary was the Apache chieftain Geronimo. But it was Sitting Bull who won the Indians' most prominent victory against the U.S. Army, when several thousand Native American warriors surrounded and defeated the forces commanded by the vainglorious General George A. Custer along the Little Bighorn River on June 25-26, 1876, killing 268 American soldiers—only days before the U.S. celebrated the centennial of the Declaration of Independence.

Born around 1831 in the Dakota Territory, Sitting Bull fought in many of the long-running battles between white settlers and Indians, from the early 1860s through the early 1870s. Still the white wave rolled on, as railroads sought to build tracks across Indian lands and a gold rush in Dakota brought thousands of prospectors into the region.

Sitting Bull's victory over Custer prompted retaliation by Washington, and the chief and his followers fled to Canada, where they lived in dire poverty; in 1881, the Indians accepted a government offer to return to the U.S., where Sitting Bull served two years in jail before he was released. By now he had achieved notoriety for his 1876 triumph, and he lived as a celebrity, meeting President Grover Cleveland and appearing briefly in Buffalo Bill Cody's Wild West Show. But when the last spasm of Indian resistance emerged in the late 1880s—the delusional Ghost Dance movement—whites again feared Sitting Bull's influence. Federal officials ordered the chief's arrest, and he was killed in the melee that ensued. A final indignity remained: Sitting Bull's cabin was torn down and rebuilt as an attraction at the Chicago World's Fair of 1893.

Voice of Freedom: 1809-65

HIS STORY SEEMS HEWN AS MUCH from legend and folklore as from history: a rawboned youth from the backwoods of the American frontier, he rose to guide his nation through a bloody Civil War that ended its reliance on human slavery, kept its Union intact and restored its founding vision—only to die at the hand of an assassin as the war ended.

His success story embodies the American Dream: entirely self-taught, he worked his father's farm; rode flatboats down the Mississippi River; served briefly in the Black Hawk Indian War; then moved to Springfield, Ill., where he studied law, married well and began a long career as a regional lawyer, riding a judicial circuit on horseback. Elected to Congress in 1846, he opposed a trumped-up U.S. war with Mexico and lost favor with his constituents, then retired from politics until the nation's rising tensions over slavery lured him back into public life in the mid-1850s.

Lincoln became the most articulate voice against human bondage in the nation, earning wide respect in a failed Senate campaign in 1858, then using his new fame to win the nomination of the antislavery Republican Party in 1860. His election brought the secession of 11 states in the South, but he stood firm, rallying the unprepared North to a final battle over the future of the Union. Cursed with a parade of weak generals (at right, he meets with General George McClellan in 1862), he taught himself military strategy and gradually found generals who could fight.

A masterly politician, Lincoln held the Union cause together through a long and bloody conflict. In the wake of the war's pivotal battle, he rearticulated the nation's values in his powerful Gettysburg Address. After winning a second term, he pledged the Union would welcome the seceded states back "with malice toward none, with charity for all." He was slain just after the Confederacy surrendered, but his mighty task was done.

Abraham Lincoln

Capital's Cassandra: 1818-83

Karl Marx

KARL MARX'S DAMNING CRITIQUE of capitalism played an outsize role in world history for a century after his death. After tangling with authorities in his native Germany, the young economist moved to Paris in 1843, and the French revolts of 1830, 1848 and 1871 strongly influenced his thinking on class struggle and revolution. He moved to London in 1849 and spent the last 34 years of his life there, much of it in the British Museum, where he wrote the majority of his best-known works, including most of *Das Kapital,* his masterwork.

Marx's utopian socialist dreams proved dead wrong, devolving into the horrors of communist Russia and China. But his predictions about capitalism were prescient in his own time and are surprisingly relevant today. Marx, to put it more simply than he himself ever did, saw the market logic of capitalism as producing recurring, ever more dangerous crises, precisely because of its tendency to channel most of the riches created by society into the pockets of a wealthy élite who seek to increase profits by cutting costs, i.e., wages—leaving growing numbers of people no longer able to afford products, thus forcing a contraction of the economy. Sound familiar? Anticipating the 99%, Marx aimed to Occupy Wall Street more than a 150 years ago.

V.I. Lenin

Titan of Revolution: 1870-1924

HE WAS THE INITIATOR OF THE central drama—the tragedy—of the 20th century, the rise of totalitarian states. A bookish man with a scholar's habits and a general's tactical instinct, V.I. Lenin (a pseudonym for V.I. Ulyanov) introduced the practice of taking an all-embracing ideology and imposing it on an entire society rapidly and mercilessly. He created a regime that erased politics, erased historical memory, erased opposition. In his short career in power, from 1917 until his death in 1924, Lenin created a model not merely for his successor, Joseph Stalin, but for Mao Zedong, for Adolf Hitler, for Pol Pot.

The signal event of Lenin's youth came when his eldest brother was hanged for conspiring to help assassinate Czar Alexander III. As a lawyer, Lenin became involved in radical politics; at first he was a pedant, the journalist-scholar who married Marxist theory to an incisive analysis of insurrectionist tactics. After Russia's royal regime fell in 1917, his Bolshevik party was primed to step into the power vacuum and take over.

Leading the new state, Lenin explored his perverse reading of the Enlightenment view of man as modeling clay and sought to create a new template for human nature and behavior through social engineering of the most radical kind. It was Lenin who built the first concentration camps; who set off artificial famine as a political weapon; who disbanded the last vestige of democratic government; who waged war on the intelligentsia and on religious believers, wiping out any traces of civil liberty and a free press. Lenin reshaped Russia—not into his dream state—but into a corrupt and failing dictatorship.

—*By David Remnick*

People and Party—United! *A 1957 poster salutes the 40th anniversary of the revolution*

1917-1957
В БОРЬБЕ –
ЗА СОВЕТСКУЮ ВЛАСТЬ.
ЗА НАШУ СОВЕТСКУЮ РОДИНУ
КОММУНИЗМ –
НАРОД И ПАРТИЯ – ЕДИНЫ!

Emmeline Pankhurst

Suffrage Crusader: 1858-1928

NOT EVEN THE NOISIEST VOICES arguing that women's "proper place" is in the home could seriously suggest today that they should not have the vote. Yet "the mother half of the human family," in Emmeline Pankhurst's phrase, was not fully enfranchised until the 20th century. In Britain, universal suffrage was granted only in the year of her death, 1928. The struggle to get votes for women, led by Mrs. Pankhurst and her daughter Christabel, who headed the militant suffragists, convulsed Britain from 1905 to 1914. The opposition the Liberal government put up is incomprehensible today, and it provoked, among all classes and conditions of women, furious and passionate protests. Women were battered in demonstrations and, on hunger strikes, brutally force-fed in prison. When these measures risked taking lives, the infamous Cat and Mouse Act was passed so that a dangerously weakened hunger striker would be released and then rearrested when strong enough to continue her sentence. Under its terms, Mrs. Pankhurst, age 54 in 1912, went to prison 12 times that year.

Her husband Richard supported her cause; when he died suddenly in 1898, she was left to bring up her children alone, with no private means. She and two of her daughters formed an intrepid, determined, powerfully gifted band. In 1903 they founded the Women's Social and Political Union, adopting a French Revolutionary sense of public spectacle and symbolic ceremony to win their goal. The political leaders of Edwardian Britain were utterly confounded by the energy and violence of this female rebellion. Joan of Arc was the suffragists' mascot, Boadicea their goddess, and Mrs. Pankhurst the true inheritor of the armed maidens of heroic legend.

—By Marina Warner

Lift-off *Pankhurst is removed from a London rally in 1912. British women won the right to vote in 1928, eight years after U.S. women did so*

Freedom Fighter: 1879-1966

BORN INTO AN IRISH WORKING-class family, Margaret Sanger witnessed her mother's slow death, worn out after 18 pregnancies and 11 live births. While working as a practical nurse and midwife in the poorest neighborhoods of New York City before World War I, she saw women deprived of their health, sexuality and ability to care for children already born. Contraceptive information was suppressed by clergy-influenced, physician-accepted laws. Yet the educated had access to such information and products.

This injustice inspired Sanger to defy church and state. In a series of articles called "What Every Girl Should Know," then in her own newspaper *The Woman Rebel* and through local clinics that dispensed woman-controlled forms of birth control (a phrase she coined), she put information and power into the hands of women. Her brave and joyous life included fulfilling work, three children, two husbands, many lovers and a large network of friends and colleagues. Indeed, she lived as if she and everyone else had the right to control her or his own life. By word and deed, she pioneered the most radical, humane and transforming political movement of the 20th and 21st centuries.

—By Gloria Steinem

Margaret Sanger

85

Germany *Adolf Hitler basks in the adoration of a crowd at a Harvest Festival in Bückeburg in 1937*

Fanatical Fascist: 1889-1945

MORE THAN 65 YEARS AFTER Adolf Hitler committed suicide in a bunker amid the ashes of his capital city, Berlin, the world still struggles to explain every aspect of his rampage through the chronicles of history. How, amid a century when science and technology showered abundant gifts on mankind, could a monster have risen to power by harnessing impulses that reeked of the Dark Ages: tribal pride, racial and ethnic bigotry, mass murder, an intimidating reign of terror.

Yet rise he did, harnessing the frustration and rage of the German people, humiliated by their defeat in World War I and impoverished by economic depression. Despite their thuggishness, his National Socialist Party followers possessed in spades what other Germans seemed to lack: purpose, energy, belief, a cause. Hitler did not seize power; he rose legally, becoming Chancellor in 1933 and instituting the techniques that we now call fascist: a tightly controlled press; the use of ethnic scapegoats to build majority support; a mutually beneficial alliance among industry, the army and government; the co-optation of religious leaders; the use of diplomatic crises and foreign wars to create national unity.

It worked. With the growing consent of the public, Hitler's aggressive diplomacy brought Germany's neighbors under its sway through bluff and bluster. Military aggression followed: when Hitler declared war on Poland on Sept. 1, 1939, Europe was plunged into its greatest war. But Hitler, a classic demagogue, allowed his visions of glory to trump his common sense. When he declared war on his ally of convenience, Joseph Stalin's Soviet Union, he embroiled himself in a two-front war that ended in the destruction of Berlin, Germany and its Führer. At war's end, the liberation of Hitler's vast network of death camps— where 6 million Jews were murdered in the Holocaust—revealed the extent of his madness, and he joined the list of history's most murderous and malignant monsters.

Adolf Hitler

Britain's Bulwark: 1874-1965

WINSTON CHURCHILL CAME OF a military dynasty. His ancestor John Churchill had been named first Duke of Marlborough in 1702 for his many victories in Continental wars. As a young man of undistinguished academic accomplishment, Winston entered the army as a cavalry officer. He took enthusiastically to soldiering, then became a foreign correspondent. He was to write all his life, eventually winning a Nobel Prize for Literature. Writing, however, never fully engaged his energies. Politics consumed him. His father Randolph had been a brilliant political failure; Winston aimed to succeed where his father had not.

He entered Parliament in 1901 at age 26. In 1904 he left the Conservative Party to join the Liberals. Theirs was the coming party, and in its ranks he soon achieved high office. He became Home Secretary in 1910 and First Lord of the Admiralty in 1911. In charge of the navy in World War I, he initiated a major effort to outflank the Germans on the Western Front with a 1915 attack at Gallipoli on the Mediterranean. It was a heroic failure that forced Churchill's resignation and led to his political eclipse. But by espousing anti-Nazi policies in his wilderness years between 1933 and 1939, he ensured that when the moment of final confrontation between Britain and Hitler came in 1940, he stood out as the one man in whom the nation could place its trust.

His was a bleak inheritance. Yet he inspired his people with stirring speeches, committed British troops to a daring plan to open a second front against the Axis Powers in North Africa, helped bring the U.S. into the war and even accepted his enemy Joseph Stalin as an ally against Hitler. Yet just as the Allies defeated Hitler, Churchill's party lost the general election. He returned to power in 1951 and led Britain for four more years, though his best days were behind him. His name endures as the greatest of Britain's war leaders, and all free men and women are in his debt.

—By John Keegan

Winston Churchill

Britain *Prime Minister Winston Churchill visits a London street bombed by Germany in 1941*

Democracy's Defender: 1882-1945

THE SECOND WORLD WAR FOUND democracy fighting for its life. By 1941 there were only a dozen or so democratic states left on earth. But great leadership emerged in time to rally the democratic cause. Future historians, looking back at the bloody 20th century, will likely regard Franklin Delano Roosevelt as the leader most responsible for mobilizing democratic energies and faith, first against economic collapse and then against military terror.

F.D.R. was the best-loved and most hated U.S. President of the 20th century. He was loved because, though patrician by birth, upbringing and style, he believed in and fought for plain people—for the "forgotten man" (and woman), for the "third of the nation, ill-housed, ill-clad, ill-nourished." He was loved because he radiated personal charm, joy in his work, optimism for the future.

But he was hated too—hated because he called for change, and the changes he proposed reduced the power, status, income and self-esteem of those who profited most from the old order. For decades, his New Deal reforms were accepted as familiar, benign and beneficial, although in recent years such government-run social programs have again come under critical scrutiny.

He was not a perfect man. In the service of his objectives, he could be devious, guileful, manipulative, underhanded, even ruthless. But he had great strengths. He relished wielding power and rejoiced in party combat. He was a realist in means but an idealist in ends. Above all, F.D.R. stood for humanity against ideology; against the totalitarians' love of abstractions, he wanted to find practical ways to help decent men and women make a better world for themselves and their children. An optimist who fought his own brave way back from polio, he brought confidence and hope to a frightened and stricken nation.

Franklin D. Roosevelt

Victor *Roosevelt visits Georgia with daughter Anna and wife Eleanor prior to his 1933 inauguration*

Mao Zedong

Resist! *Mao addresses the People's Army circa 1939, urging opposition to invading Japanese forces*

Tyrant in Disguise: 1893-1976

MAO ZEDONG WAS BORN INTO A China that was falling apart; he united it with bonds of fear and blood. The fading Qing dynasty could not contain the nation's spiraling social and economic unrest; China had mortgaged its revenues and natural resources to foreign powers. Mao's earliest surviving essay, written at 19, concerned an ancient Chinese exponent of realpolitik, the fearsome 4th century B.C. administrator Shang Yang, famed for instituting a set of ruthlessly enforced laws designed "to punish the wicked and rebellious, in order to preserve the rights of the people."

In the decades to come, Mao became a modern-day Shang Yang, fighting a host of foes to realize his vision. His enemies were legion: the Nationalist Party, led by Chiang Kai-shek, who fought Mao's Communist rebels for control of the nation; the Japanese, who tried to smash his base in northern China in the late 1930s;

his Communist Party rivals, who attacked the coalition he forged with the Nationalists to counter Japan's invasion; landlords, who hated his pro-peasant rhetoric and activism.

Mao finally defeated Chiang and proclaimed the People's Republic in Beijing in 1949. As China's leader, he fought against the U.S. in the Korean War and battled with Soviet leader Nikita Khrushchev after he denounced Joseph Stalin. Most memorably, Mao unleashed his brainwashed young minions, the Red Guards, against a host of his enemies in the Cultural Revolution he led from 1966-76.

Along the way, Mao lost his humanity. He used famine as an instrument of policy, he fomented endless waves of party terror and he built a grim totalitarian state based around his cult of personality. Only after his death has the full extent of his crimes begun to emerge. Hailed as a leader who loved the people, this corrupt tyrant quashed his people's rights.

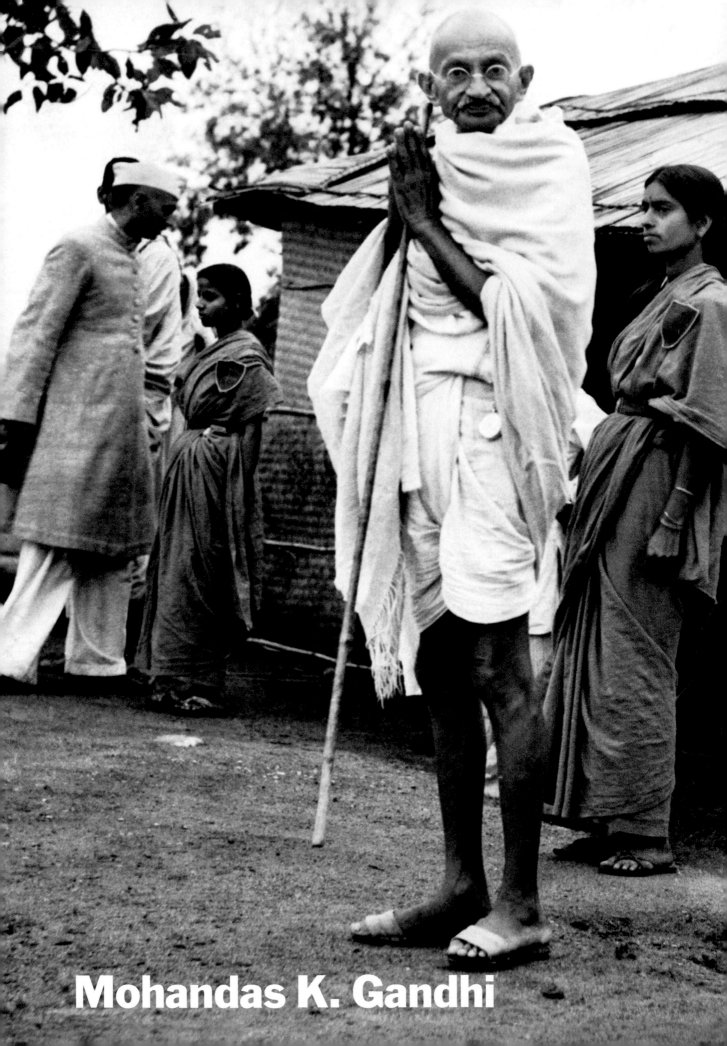

Mohandas K. Gandhi

India's Liberator: 1869-1948

NOT SINCE THE BIBLICAL TALE OF David and Goliath had two contenders seemed more mismatched. On one side stood the mighty British Empire, the most sprawling imperial realm in history. On the other stood the skinny, homely man on the left, Mohandas K. Gandhi. The rivals' epic duel over the future of India ran for four decades, and it ended with Britain's decision to grant sovereignty to India, a signal that European colonialism had run its course.

Voltaire had fought a stagnant French regime by the power of his words, moving public opinion in his direction. Gandhi went a step further, forging a template that human-rights activists everywhere would soon adopt: he created a strong intellectual case for his demand for India's freedom, staged events of civil disobedience that deliberately dramatized the inequities of British rule, employed women and children effectively as soldiers in his protest army, refused to engage in violence against his foes and used mass media to circulate his message. He turned himself into the visual symbol of those for whom he fought, adopting the clothing, bearing and humble lifestyle of India's poorest citizens.

Gandhi became an activist as a young lawyer who had emigrated from India to South Africa. In that highly racist society, he was regarded as a "colored" and granted second-class status (native blacks were third-class citizens). There he learned the basic tools of protest, which he began to apply in his homeland after his return in 1915. Fighting not only against British hegemony but also against India's caste system, its oppression of women and its inequities of religion, class and wealth, he staged marches, rallies and protests that won world attention. When TIME named him Man of the Year for 1930, he was penned up in an Indian jail. After World War II, an exhausted Britain finally gave in to his demands: India achieved its independence in 1947, only to succumb to a brutal civil war between Hindus and Muslims, ending in the nation's partition. When he died at the hands of a Hindu assassin early in 1948, Gandhi's dream had been realized—but sadly, it was purchased in blood.

American Dreamer: 1929-68

Martin Luther King Jr.

TAKING HIS MARCHING ORDERS directly from Mohandas Gandhi, the Rev. Martin Luther King Jr. became the public face—and the eloquent voice—of the movement for black civil rights in the U.S. The son of a Georgia preacher, he followed in his father's footsteps, becoming pastor of a congregation in Montgomery, Ala. It was there, in the mid-1950s, that he emerged as a leader in the struggle for black equality, as he led the 385-day long strike against the city bus company's segregationist policies. By the time of his assassination in 1968, King's crusade to win equal rights for U.S. blacks had largely been won, legislated into law by two historic civil rights acts. Yet he did more, helping free whites from the burden of their dishonorable prejudices.

How did he do it? As a preacher, he spoke in biblical cadences ideally suited to leading a stride toward freedom that found inspiration in Old Testament tales of the Israelites. His ministry put him in touch with the black masses in their churches, strongest of America's black institutions. He was a man of physical courage whose belief in nonviolence never wavered—even when his home was bombed, with his wife and children inside. His eloquence equalled Lincoln's as he urged Americans to embrace his dream of a land where all are judged by the content of their character rather than the color of their skin.

Happy warrior *Mandela visits a school in 1993, two years after his release from prison*

Slayer of Apartheid: 1918-

ISTORY'S MOVERS AND SHAKERS are not always lovable. But in 2012, as this book went to press, a kindly great-grandfather in South Africa with a disarming smile, a fondness for gaudy shirts and a Nobel Peace Prize on his mantel was clearly among the most admired and beloved figures on the planet. His name was Nelson Mandela; he was 94 years old, and the entire world knew what the first lines of his obituary would read: Imprisoned for 27 years at the hands of a hatefully racist regime, he emerged from prison not to berate his captors but to forgive them. He then helped engineer South Africa's transition to a fully inclusive state, becoming the first black President of South Africa in an election in which his fellow black citizens voted for the first time.

Mandela's tale constitutes a hero's journey worthy of Joseph Campbell. It began with his birth into a high-ranking family in the Tembu culture of the great Xhosa tribe. Bright and capable from an early age, Rolihlahla Mandela received a good education in a British Methodist school and, along the way, acquired a new name: Nelson. After graduating from college, he tangled with his guardian, refusing to take part in an arranged marriage, and moved to Johannesburg. There he encountered the full weight of South Africa's brutal system of apartheid, which consigned native blacks to third-class status and forced them to reside in bogus, poverty-stricken "homelands."

Mandela became a noted attorney and a capable defender of black rights, but he became slowly radicalized by official oppression. Once a Gandhi-style pacifist, he left his law practice, went underground and led a group devoted to guerrilla resistance. In 1962 he was apprehended; in 1964 he went to prison, where he soon became the invisible yet inescapable symbol of South Africa's repression.

As the nation's society crumbled, crime ran rampant and its standing in the world was diminished, until at last the regime was forced to free its iconic foe. On Feb. 11, 1990, Mandela was released from prison, in one of the great moral and political victories of the 20th century. As he left the jail, South Africa experienced a new dawn of freedom; then, as President Mandela, he began the reconciliation of his nation's races, a process still in progress.

Others Who Turned History's Tide
A general, a conqueror and a terrorist reshaped their worlds

Julius Caesar
100-44 B.C.

Nobly born, Caesar served as a soldier in Asia when he was 18, earned a medal for bravery, then returned to Rome, where he climbed nimbly up the ladder of power. He curried favor with Crassus, Rome's richest man, and married off his daughter to Pompey, Rome's most powerful man. Seeking fame in arms, he was 41 when he began his conquest of Gaul, yet he became a genius of military speed and surprise, extending Rome's reign across all of Gaul, into Britain and across the Rhine.

When Crassus died, Pompey and Caesar vied for power, and Pompey's Senate allies ordered Caesar not to return to Rome. But Caesar defied them and crossed the Rubicon into Italy, where he pursued and defeated Pompey's forces. After a cowed Senate proclaimed him dictator, Caesar began an ambitious program of reforms, but a cabal of nobles saw his grasp on power as a threat and conspired to murder him in the Senate on the Ides of March, 44 B.C.

Tamerlane
1336-1405

The English, who lived far from his conquests, still trembled at the name. of Tamerlane "The scourge of God," Christopher Marlowe quailed nearly 200 years after the death of the military genius from outside Samarkand. When the city of Isfahan defied him, Tamerlane slaughtered 70,000 of its inhabitants and raised a pyramid of heads.

More accurately known as Timur-i-Lang ("Timur the Lame," for an arrow wound to the heel), the warlord loved beauty as much as war and turned Samarkand into a wonder of the world. But his first love was conquest, and he ranks with Alexander and Genghis Khan as one of history's greatest empire builders: he defeated the Golden Horde of Central Asia, the Ottoman Turks of the Middle East, the Delhi Sultanate of the subcontinent and the Mamluks of Egypt. He is thought to have overseen the deaths of some 17 million people, at a time when the act of killing was up close and personal.

Osama bin Laden
1957-2011

It cannot be denied that his deeds shook the world: the terrorist attack he unleashed on the U.S. on Sept. 11, 2001, was stunning in its planning and in its brutality, killing some 3,000 civilians. But the great war Osama bin Laden hoped to ignite between the Christian West and the Muslim world never materialized: the terrorist's vision of a world ruled by fundamentalist mullahs was out of step with modern times, while his tactics were abhorrent.

Son of a wealthy contractor with ties to the Saudi royal family, bin Laden was radicalized as a young man and honed his hatred for the West fighting as a *mujahedin* against Soviet troops in Afghanistan in the 1980s. Outraged by the presence of American troops in Saudi Arabia during the first Gulf War, bin Laden led a number of successful terrorist attacks against the U.S. and its allies but was driven into hiding after 9/11. He was hunted down and killed by U.S. Navy SEALs in May 2011.

Architects of

Culture

They also transformed our world, through their imaginative vision, through the exhilarating power of their art, through the values they expressed in their works. They are the creators.

From left: *Self Portrait,* Pablo Picasso; *Vitruvian Man,* Leonardo da Vinci; *Don Quixote and Sancho,* Alexandre Decamps; Louis Armstrong

Poetry's Father
c. 9th century B.C.

THE TWO GREAT EPICS ATTRIB-
uted to Homer originated as oral
poems in preliterate Greece. The
Iliad tells of the wrath of Achilles
and the siege and fall of Troy to the Greeks
in the Trojan War, while the *Odyssey* relates
the journeys of the warrior Odysseus as
he returns to his home in Greece after the
war. Alive with rich language, bristling with
marvelous incidents and penetrating in their
understanding of human nature, these poems
have earned their place on the bookshelf for
centuries. Far from academic texts, they are
robust, entertaining works of art.

Homer's characters—the Cyclops, Odysseus,
the Sirens, Achilles, Patroclus and Hector—
were first brought to memorable life by
roving singers. Homer (or the gaggle of bards
given that name) did not wander around
Greece with 12,109 lines of the *Odyssey*
committed to memory. Instead, the familiar
repetitions—all those "wine-dark seas" and
"rosy-fingered dawns"—were actually stock
phrases, allowing the bard to fill out his line of
verse and move the story along. The two tales'
power endures: recent translations by the late
Princeton professor Robert Fagles were best
sellers. Fagles told TIME's Paul Gray that he
believed, despite scholars' views, that Homer
did exist and shaped his epics from a long oral
tradition. "It's awfully hard to prove," he said,
"but I'm an incurable romantic."

Homer

Sophocles

Titan of Tragedy: c. 496-406 B.C.

READING GREEK TRAGEDIES ON the page, we may admire the power and insight of their authors. But to see the theaters where these works were staged—vast spaces, often perched in the most impressive of settings, like the theater in the sacred city of Delphi shown here, where the plays were performed by masked actors under the harsh vertical rays of the sun—is to understand the audacity and majesty of the Greek conception of drama.

Beginning in the Victorian era, these powerful, emotionally charged works were too often staged as refined pageants. Directors handed out masks, wrote long program notes about catharsis and advised their puzzled charges to express hubris, which often left them looking like damaged Roman coins. In the 1960s, the coin flipped to the other side, as directors began staging the tragedies as love-ins, mosh pits and Occupy Thebes encampments.

No matter: Greek tragedies, like Shakespeare, benefit from a good shake-up. Sadly, the works of only three tragedians—Aeschylus, Sophocles and Euripides—have survived. Aeschylus, the elder of the three, offers tragedy at its most primal in his three-part masterpiece, *The Oresteia,* while Euripides' gripping, sexy tale of Dionysian possession, *The Bacchae,* remains a favorite with modern audiences. But Sophocles' plays are most often staged. His *Oedipus Rex* is a titanic, moving account of a flawed ruler who is blinded by stubborn pride—and then by his own hand. *Antigone*, a stirring story of the individual pitted against the power of the state, never loses its relevance. After more than two thousand years, the plays of Sophocles are brimful of life.

Comedy Writer: 1265-1321

THE MOTHER OF DANTE ALIGHIERI, not long before his birth, had a dream in which her son, having eaten the berries of a laurel tree, grew up and was miraculously transformed into a shimmering peacock. The portent was fulfilled in a blaze of genius for which the brilliant bird is an apt metaphor. For seven centuries *The Divine Comedy,* which in 14,233 lines of lordly language describes the poet's descent into hell and ascent into heaven through the refining fires of purgatory, has been widely considered the greatest poem ever composed.

At one level, *La DivinaCommedia* is a spiritual autobiography; at another, a parable of the progress of the soul; at a third, one of the noblest love stories ever told. Incidentally it is a manual of mysticism and an encyclopedia of Greek, Hebrew, Arabic and Scholastic learning. Written in vernacular Italian rather than Latin, it reached a wide audience and rejected the church's grip on the arts. The long poem straddles epochs, at once a journey through medieval theology and the gospel of a rising religion of individuality that replaced it. Exploring the great questions of man's essence and existence, it has retained its relevance across the centuries.

Born in Florence in a turbulent age, Dante himself was "somewhat presumptuous, disdainful and haughty," according to a contemporary. He idolized from afar his crush object, thought to be Beatrice Portinari, with the ardor encouraged by Eleanor of Aquitaine's court. He also sought political power, but he sided with the wrong faction amid Florence's raging civic wars and was exiled from his hometown; it was during this period that he wrote his masterwork. Grudges die hard in Italy; a mayor of Florence finally revoked the city's ban on its greatest writer—in 2008.

Afterlife *In this detail from a 1465 portrait of Dante by Domenico di Michelino, Florence's Il Duomo is on the right; hell and the mountain of Purgatory are on the left, and heaven is above*

Chivalry's Patron: 1122-1204

WED TO TWO KINGS, MOTHER OF two more, Queen of both France and England and a patron of the arts who fostered the birth of chivalry, Eleanor of Aquitaine became one of the most influential women in history. Duchess of Aquitaine and Countess of Poitiers at 15, she married King Louis VII of France and took part in the Second Crusade, then arranged to have her marriage to the pious, monkish Louis annulled. After quickly marrying Henry Plantagenet, who became King Henry II of England the next year, she bore eight children, including future kings Richard the Lionheart and King John, signer of the Magna Carta.

Brisk, bright, determined and capable, Eleanor helped Henry II reshape both England and France. But her effect on culture was as strong as her political heft: estranged from Henry in 1168, she set up her own court in Poitiers, where, in sunny arcades, to the sound of strings and flutes, the lover of the arts nurtured the young cult of chivalric romance and the idealization of the feminine, conferring new power and respect upon all Europe's women. She governed England while son Richard was on crusade, and died at 82, having transformed the politics and culture of her era.

Eleanor of Aquitaine

QVE ANIMO CVNCTA POETA SVO ⁓ DOCTVS ADEST DANTES SVA QVEM FLORENTIA SAEPE
EVA NOCERE POETAE ⁓ QVEM VIVVM VIRTVS CARMEN IMAGO FACIT

Dante Alighieri

Leonardo da Vinci

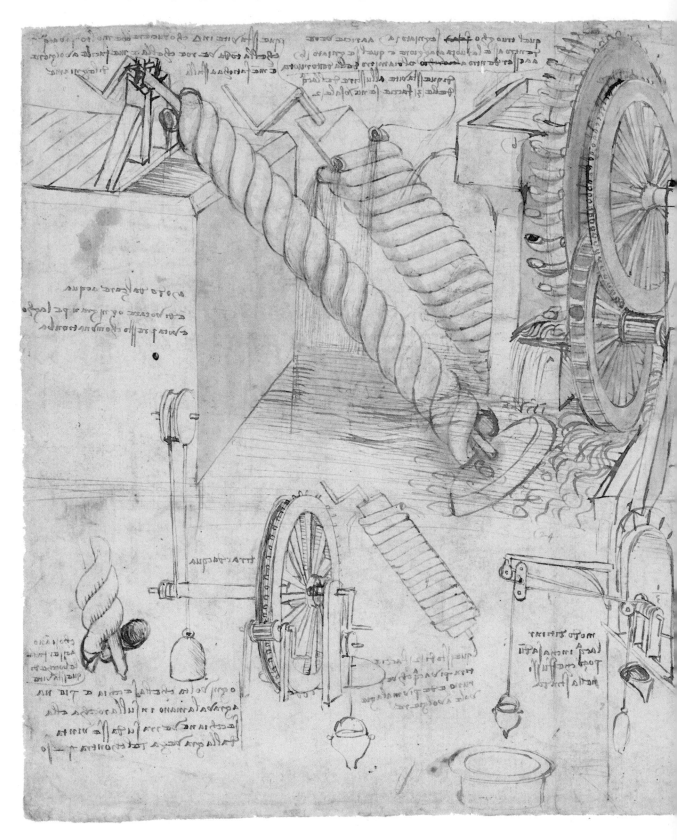

Prodigious Polymath: 1452-1519

BRITISH ART HISTORIAN KEN-neth Clark called Leonardo da Vinci "the great Sphinx of art history," but he was also its great Rorschach blot. The modern world has seen almost as many Leonardos as there are *Léonardistes.* Magus, "Renaissance man," supergay, world's first nonlinear thinker—the parade of stereotypes marches on. Though Leonardo was chemist and physicist, mechanical engineer, musician, architect, anatomist and botanist as well as painter, it is not wholly possible to draw a dividing line between art and science in his work. Painting was to him a method of inquiry into the world's structure; it was the empiricism of sight itself. His scientific work was presented in drawings of ravishing subtlety. Their purely descriptive intent in no way affects their aesthetic power.

Many artists in the Renaissance worked, as Leonardo did, in a wide variety of media: drawing, painting, sculpture and architecture. None, however, had Leonardo's astounding and insatiable curiosity about the makeup and governing laws of the physical world. One of the striking things about the machines in his notebooks—like those of the *Codex Atlanticus* (1478-1518), at left—is how they prefigure the future of formal engineering draftsmanship without becoming schematic diagrams.

Leonardo the man was conflicted, contradictory, almost incredibly hard to get at, to or around. Though a great deal is known about his work, it survives only in fragments. His big projects for sculpture were never completed; his major mural commemorating a Florentine victory, the Battle of Anghiari, became a blistered wreck and was painted over. Little survives of his *Last Supper* in Milan. He never found time to edit the intriguing but amorphous mass of his writings into coherent treatises And so the melancholy catalog of ruin and loss goes on. Yet even seen through a glass, darkly, he could draw like an angel, and he was unquestionably the greatest observer of the real world in his time.

—By Robert Hughes

Niccolò Machiavelli

THIS VOLUME RECORDS THE deeds of spiritual leaders, high-minded philosophers and heroic rebels. But in Niccolò Machiavelli we encounter a mind resolutely focused on this world and attuned more to political advancement than spiritual growth. Machiavelli offered a famously dim view of human nature in *The Prince,* his influential treatise on leadership, written in 1513. People are so "ungrateful, fickle, [and] false," he wrote, that a ruler should comfortably abandon conventional morality in dealing with them. He should slay deposed rulers and their families; recognize that friendship "yields nothing"; and, beneath a veneer of compassion and honesty, master treachery and deceit. In short, because man is evil, leaders must know "how to do evil."

Such coldhearted prescriptions have shaped Machiavelli's reputation as the grand master of brutal pragmatism. But they reveal surprisingly little about the man himself—a statesman, poet, playwright and Florentine patriot. In a lively 2007 biography, *Machiavelli: Philosopher of Power,* Ross King argues that the amoral tone of Machiavelli's work reflects his age more than his temperament and reveals a person who is richly human and surprisingly sympathetic.

In the 16th century, gore and tragedy dominated the Italian peninsula, a hodge-podge of warring city-states, kingdoms and republics. Machiavelli roamed this minefield of intrigue on horseback as Florence's diplomatic envoy from the age of 29, encountering a henchman trained in strangulation and a ruler who ate his brother-in-law's heart. After Florence fell to Spain in 1512, Machiavelli was imprisoned, tortured and driven into exile. Even so, in his *Discourses* (1517), he demonstrated a more idealistic outlook, embracing personal liberty, republicanism and good government.

—*By William Lee Adams*

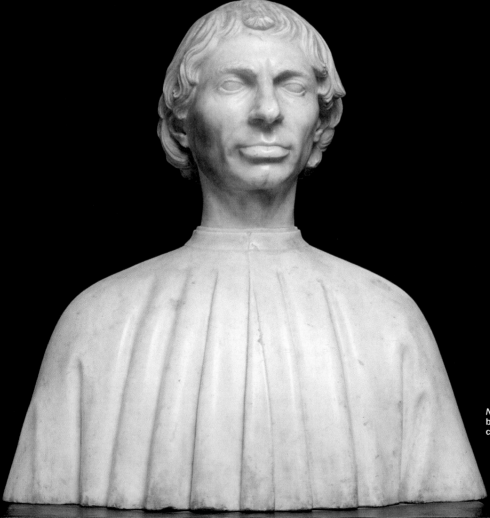

Nicolò Machiavelli,
by Antonio del Pollaiuolo,
c. 1465

Michelangelo with Turban
by Giuliano Bugiardini,
1522

Master of Arts: 1475-1564

HISTORY'S GREATEST SCULPTOR, it turns out, did a little painting on the side. Born in Florence at the right time—the high period of the Italian Renaissance—Michelangelo Buonarroti was a prodigy whose command of drawing brought him attention at an early age. He was apprenticed to the studio of the noted artist Domenico Ghirlandaio, but within a year the master himself was making jealous noises at his protégé. Lorenzo de' Medici, the Florentine dictator and patron, was so impressed with the boy's genius that he adopted him and educated him as one of his own sons.

By age 28, Michelangelo had sculpted one of his greatest works, the magnificent *David*. "I saw the angel in the marble," he declared, "and carved until I set him free." For the next 60 years, he oscillated between Rome and Florence and among demanding patrons, including Pope Julius II, who put him to work on designing a massive memorial to himself

and later to painting the ceiling of the Sistine Chapel. The Pope gave the painter no peace, showering him with questions and suggestions; once Julius II beat the painter with his cane. Michelangelo groused in a poem: "This place is wrong for me, and I'm no painter." Generations of visitors have disagreed, especially in recent years, when viewers see Michelangelo's great frescoes restored to their original brilliance, thanks to a long-overdue cleaning. As TIME art critic Robert Hughes noted, "Out of grime, a domain of light."

Michelangelo's great rival was Leonardo da Vinci: the former was by far the greater artist, the latter a more inquisitive polymath. Impassioned, striving, infatuated with the human body and struggling to give expression to superhuman forms, Michelangelo could be rude to individuals, but *"Il Divino"* was beloved for his majestic works. When he died, it took three funerals to exhaust Italy's grief: one in Rome, two in Florence.

Michelangelo

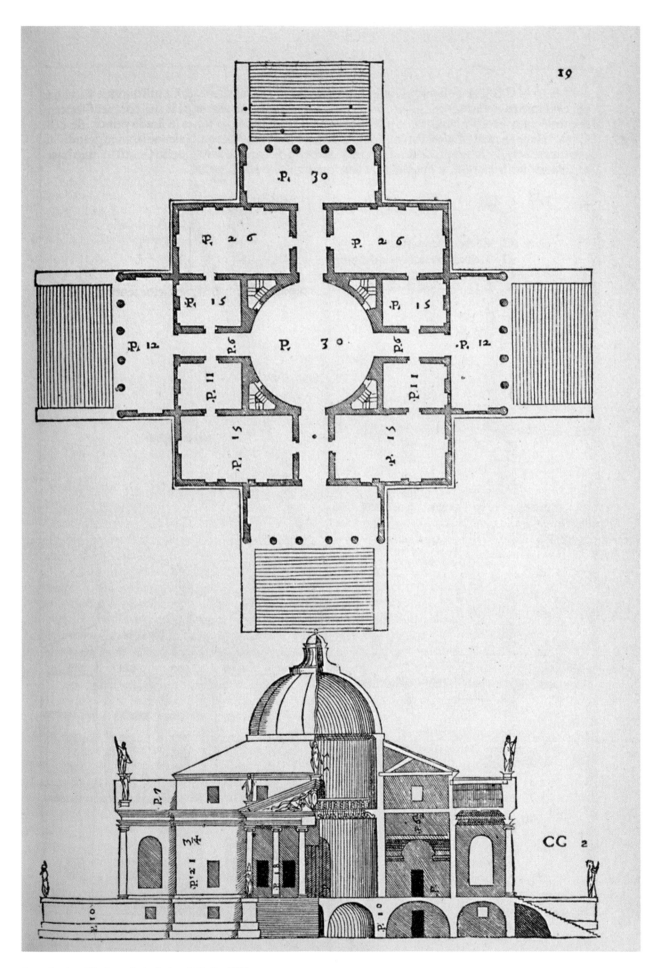

Cross-Section, Villa Rotunda, by Andrea Palladio, 1570

Palladio

Master Architect: 1508-80

PALLADIO: THE VERY NAME IS suggestive, evoking pedimented villas on the banks of the foggy Brenta, the symmetrical façade of Venice's great church, Il Redentore, and white porticos glimpsed through Deep South veils of Spanish moss. He is the most imitated architect in history; even today his name remains synonymous with flawless precision and proportion. He was, and still is, the Mozart of his profession. Andrea Palladio built nothing outside northern Italy, and several of his greatest houses stand in tracts of the Venetian countryside that must have been almost inaccessible to travelers in the 17th and 18th centuries. Yet his principles were studied as avidly in Stockholm and St. Petersburg as they were by Thomas Jefferson in Virginia and by élite English architects like Inigo Jones, William Kent and Lord Burlington. By 1850, two continents were dotted with Palladian structures.

An illiterate stone mason from Padua, Palladio was adopted as a protégé by the wealthy Gian Giorgio Trissino, who took him on several journeys to Rome. There, awed by the half-buried ruins, Palladio began the long research that would turn him into the leading architectural theorist of his age. The result was his *Four Books of Architecture,* which were published in 1570 and spread his influence throughout the West. Palladio's planning is mathematics made concrete. His buildings, strict as they are, remain both exquisite and ideal, as though held in a parenthesis somewhere outside mundane history.

—*By Robert Hughes*

Visionary Novelist: 1547-1616

BORN IN ALCALA DE HENARES, not far from Madrid, Miguel de Cervantes served an Italian cardinal in Rome as a youth, where he was enchanted by the city's Classical ruins as well as its Renaissance masterpieces. The story of his life is crowded with incident and found him involved in many of the great currents of his time. He fought in the epochal Battle of Lepanto, when Europe's Catholic maritime nations defeated the primary fleet of the Ottoman Turks, surviving three gunshot wounds. He was taken prisoner by Algerian pirates for five years and was finally ransomed by his family. He served as a purveyor for the Spanish Armada, then was clapped in jail on charges of embezzling money from the state.

In his younger years Cervantes wrote poems, a pastoral romance and several plays: all were failures. He helped pioneer modern Spanish literature by satirizing his own early work, hammering the lid on the coffin of musty medieval romances with his magnificent novel of chivalry run amuck, *Don Quixote.*

Regarded as the first true modern novel, *Don Quixote* was published in two parts. Its moving, shrewd depiction of the aging knight-errant and his canny servant, Sancho Panza, is one of the great masterworks of world literature, while the writer's direct, vernacular prose style had such a clarifying impact on the evolution of modern Spanish that it is sometimes called "the language of Cervantes."

Cervantes

Principum amicitias!

Shakespeare

Power Player: 1564-1616

FEW HUMANS HAVE DEFIED TIME and death so successfully. Wherever the sun sets and curtains rise, Falstaff struts with his gorbellied wit, Bottom bumbles through the woods, wide-eyed Ophelia trembles before Hamlet's abuse, Malvolio preens in yellow stockings, and Romeo woos Juliet. In the kingliest English and with the lowest of puns, William Shakespeare's characters speak to man from mankind's heart. The playwright coined hundreds of new words that remain in the language, yet he could pack worlds into monosyllables. "To be or not to be" is man's largest question put in man's simplest words. Once uttered, they expand to fill all the space in the human mind.

A glover's son from Warwickshire, Shakespeare left his home and wife in Stratford-upon-Avon around 1587 for the big town, London, where he joined an acting company. He was a quick study in success, turning out an average of two plays a year, borrowing plots where he could find them. Elizabethan England was in a ferment, minting a new breed: the British Renaissance man. Shakespeare channeled the energy of the times into the fluid format of his outdoor theater and the "two hours' traffick of our stage." Scene followed scene without break, and the scenery might be no more than a placard reading A WOOD NEAR ATHENS. No matter: as all theater people know, Shakespeare's works *play:* they come alive when staged, a feast of delicious scenes for actors and directors.

He was not a bohemian: he bought a piece of the players' company and a share of the Globe Theatre. In 1597 he paid £60 for New Place, the second grandest house in Stratford. His son Hamnet had died in 1596, and a spate of tragedies followed: *Hamlet, Othello, Macbeth, King Lear.* He retired to Stratford around 1611 and died young, at only 52, in 1616. Seven years later, admirers published the first edition of his works, and Shakespeare returned to life. He remains active in the theater.

Gentleman *The "Cobbe portrait" (1612) is thought to be the only painting of Shakespeare made during his lifetime. Copies had survived, but the original was not discovered until 2006*

Rembrandt

Old Master: 1606-69

YOU CAN'T OFTEN COMPARE painters with writers, because of the apples-and-oranges problem of imagining links between dissimilar arts. But in the case of Rembrandt van Rijn you can, and the temptation to do it, if not carried too far, can hardly be resisted: he was the Shakespeare of 17th century painting.

Rembrandt was not a "literary" painter, as his intense devotion to the muck and glow and substance of paint attests. But he was an incomparably theatrical one. In his work, the idea of a figure painting as tableau is exchanged for that of outright drama: deep, dark backgrounds and narrative light picking out the hierarchy of character; turbulent crowd scenes; an eye for all classes, from cobblers to kings; a vast range of expression in the faces and gestures; moments of shock alternating with passages of the most lyrical eroticism, reflectiveness, inwardness. Then, too, there are the shifts of language, the rough and the smooth, and the long series of self-portraits, including *Self-Portrait at the Age of 34,* above, from 1640, which composes Rembrandt's time-lapse scrutiny of his aging, from smooth-faced boy to old potato-nosed master and incarnates the very essence of soliloquy.

—By Robert Hughes

Maestro *Elias Gottlob Haussmann's 1746 painting of Bach is the only surviving portrait of the musician created from life. Above is the first page of Bach's* Cantata 112

Magisterial Musician: 1685-1750

J.S. Bach

JOHANN SEBASTIAN BACH CAME from a long line of musicians and spent almost his entire life in Germany in the often contentious service of pompous princelings and severe Lutheran rectors. He married twice, fathered 20 children and died far more renowned for his keyboard playing than for his mostly unpublished cantatas, Masses, sonatas and concertos. In his lifetime, he enjoyed a national reputation as a virtuoso organist, yet as a composer, he attracted mostly condescending notice.

As times have changed, the world has caught up to Bach. Since his revival began in the early 19th century, he has been universally ranked among the transcendent artists of Western civilization. Choral works that he turned out for rowdy schoolboys to sing in drafty provincial churches are cherished by the world's finest choruses. Keyboard exercises that he jotted down for his students still beguile and challenge great virtuosos. Instrumental pieces that he composed to curry favor with obscure royals are judged among the glories of all chamber music.

A crystalline logic underlies all of Bach's work, one reason he is so popular with mathematicians and scientists. But his music also throbs with a living pulse; his rhythms and modulations, however controlled, evolve with a seeming spontaneity. His endlessly inventive melodies, however neatly they fit into a scheme, rise and fall and intertwine with a lyrical life of their own, charged with energy and intensity. Offering a full measure of both head and heart, Bach stands as an exemplar not only of fullness but above all, of balance.

—*By Christopher Porterfield*

Benjamin Franklin Drawing Electricity from the Sky, by Benjamin West, c. 1816

Genial Genius: 1706-90

TO UNDERSTAND BENJAMIN Franklin's historic significance, we must first rescue him from the schoolbook stereotype: a sage geezer flying kites in the rain and lecturing us about a penny saved being a penny earned. His experiments with electricity led him to invent the lightning rod (which saved countless lives, in a world made of wooden homes and buildings prone to combustion from lightning strikes). They also led him to devise the theory of positive and negative charges, christen the battery and become one of his century's foremost scientists. His inventions included the Franklin stove and the bifocal lens.

As for his *Poor Richard's Almanac* adages, they made Franklin not only a best-selling author but also the first American media mogul: printer, editor, publisher, newspaper franchiser and consolidator and controller of the first great distribution network—the U.S. Postal Service. As a statesman, Franklin played a key role in the creation of America's four founding documents and was the only person to sign them all: the Declaration of Independence (he edited Thomas Jefferson's draft), the treaty of alliance with France (which he negotiated), the peace treaty ending the Revolution (which he also negotiated) and the Constitution (he came up with the idea of a House representing the people and a Senate representing the states).

Yet Franklin remains a man of flesh, not marble. "Among the great early figures of the American Republic, Franklin, a perennial overachiever, still seems the most human," TIME's Richard Lacayo once wrote, "... not so much a founding father as a founding uncle."

Adam Smith

Capitalist Icon: 1723-90

THE EPIC POET OF ADVENTUROUS enterprise was a quiet bachelor Scotsman who was devoted to his mother and who was briefly kidnaped by Gypsies at age 4, in the only personal adventure ever to have befallen him. A classic absent-minded professor, he got out of bed one night, absorbed in thought, and wandered 15 miles in his dressing gown before coming to his senses. But the book he wrote over a period of 10 years and published in 1776 (with nifty timing) changed the world.

The 1,097 pages of *The Wealth of Nations* offered the first full description of a free economy—one in which, Smith prophesied, the drives of millions of people for personal profit, colliding against one another in an unfettered market, would produce "universal opulence which extends itself to the lowest ranks of the people." His book rapidly became a capitalist declaration of independence from the remaining shackles of feudalism and helped launch an economic revolution that has produced far more wealth than mankind had amassed in all previous history.

In Smith's view, the great motivator of economic activity is "the uniform, constant, and uninterrupted effort of every man to better his condition"—or, bluntly, self-interest. This goal expresses itself as the drive for profit and creates that great marvel, the self-regulating market, which he described as "the invisible hand." Critics, however, claim his theories are an apologia for greed. English economist Walter Bagehot offered a dissenting view: the frugal, striving Smith, he said, "thought that there was a Scotchman inside every man."

Jean-Jacques Rousseau

Founding Romantic: 1712-78

HE WAS THE FIRST MODERN MAN, and he staked his claim to that title in memorable fashion. With the publication of his *Confessions* in 1782, four years after his death, Jean-Jacques Rousseau helped strip away the veils of propriety that society had long imposed on honest self-examination. Resolving to "put his life to the test of truth," he recorded in *Confessions* every real and fancied failure, every agonizing triumph, every abrasive sand grain of guilt. The memoir shocked 18th century Europe with its author's admissions of sexual masochism and other private matters. His "sentimental" novels, in tandem with the *Confessions,* charted Europe's passage from the Enlightenment, with its emphasis on reason, into the new Romantic era, which embraced subjective feelings above all.

A Swiss from the puritan, theocratic city of Geneva, Rousseau had a checkered childhood. His mother died when he was born, while his father either spoiled him or neglected him. In his youth, he was an apprentice lawyer, an engraver, a valet and a vagrant. Around 1744, Rousseau moved to Paris, where he lived as a music copyist. Somewhere along the line, he underwent a sort of religious experience and concluded that revealing the truth about himself would reveal the truth about all men.

Rousseau's impact abides. He denounced civilization and praised the state of nature and its "noble savages." His proclamation of man's Original Goodness led to the sentimentalization of childhood, while his condemnation of private property makes him sound prepared to lead an Occupy the Bourse rally.

In 1762 he published *The Social Contract,* which posed the then astounding notion that government rests upon the consent of the governed; it helped foment the French Revolution. Its famous statement, "Man is born free and he is everywhere in chains," anticipates the thinking of Karl Marx. Yet, like so many idealists, Rousseau could not live up to his own rhetoric. His mistress bore five children to the man who venerated childhood; he sent them all to homes for foundlings.

Youth *Rousseau is depicted in his challenging early years in this 19th century French engraving*

Thomas Jefferson

American Sphinx: 1743-1826

OF ALL THE FOUNDING FATHERS, he has fared the worst at the hands of revisionists. If Thomas Jefferson has managed to keep his place on Mount Rushmore, he has been vilified almost everywhere else in recent years as a slave-owning hypocrite and racist; a political extremist; an apologist for the vicious French Revolution; and, in general, somewhat less than the genius remembered in our folklore.

The onslaught is unfair. But even ardent Jeffersonians admit that the man was an insoluble puzzle. The contradictions in his character and his ideas could be breathtaking. That the author of the Declaration of Independence not only owned and worked slaves at Monticello but kept one of them, Sally Hemings, as a mistress—fathering children with her but never freeing her or them—was merely the most dramatic of his inconsistencies. Yet he was arguably the most accomplished man who ever occupied the White House: naturalist, lawyer, musician, architect, geographer, inventor, scientist, agriculturalist, philologist.

A dozen powerful strands of the Enlightenment converged in him: a certain sky-blue clarity, an aggressive awareness of the world, a fascination with science, a mechanical vision of the universe and an obsession with mathematical precision. Many of the contradictions in his character arose from the discrepancies between such intellectual machinery and the passionate, organic disorders of life.

Jefferson helped shape America, serving in the Continental Congress, as a diplomat, as Secretary of State, as the President who made the Louisiana Purchase, as the founder of the University of Virginia. Yet his finest hour came when he was young, only 33. In the Declaration, he formulated the founding aspiration of America and what remains its best self: "We hold these truths to be self-evident, that all men are created equal … "

—*By Lance Morrow*

Ludwig van Beethoven

HIS ART SOARED WITH DRAMA and pathos; his achievement came despite debilitation and despair. Ludwig van Beethoven was born in Bonn, the son of a tempestuous father who raised his talented son to succeed Mozart and then drank himself to death. Beethoven's early compositions were for piano; his performances throughout Europe earned him acclaim as an improviser. But he was plagued with hearing problems, and after suffering a prolonged bout of depression, he relocated to a rural village outside Vienna and sought relief in composing. There he found the solace he needed and produced, over the next decade, a wealth of glorious and enduring symphonic works, as well as a wide variety of other compositions: sonatas and string quartets, a powerful opera and dozens of memorable incidental works.

Beethoven's music, bridging the catastrophic finale of the old century of his birth and the febrile promise of a brave new era, had the whiff of revolution: it destroyed the classical symphonic molds and established a new era of Romanticism. At a peak of achievement, he encountered a fate so unjust it remains hard to grasp: the great composer became almost completely deaf. Yet even as his hearing declined, sending him alternately into fits of despair and manic frenzy, Beethoven continued to create art of astonishing power. No ode is more joyous than the *Ninth Symphony's* "Ode to Joy"; no Mass is more solemn than his *Missa Solemnis;* no music is more intensely, gravely moving than his Late String Quartets.

Audacious and epic, serene and soothing, explosive and primal, the composer's works exist on the plane Michelangelo sought to achieve in his sculptures and frescoes. Always, Beethoven's works seem to embody struggle—the *Sturm und Drang* of the German Romantics—even though that struggle often resolves into moments of limpid purity and beauty. When TIME critic Michael Walsh in 2008 considered the composer's impact, it seemed appropriate that he would find his metaphor in the world of athletics: "Talk about dynasties: the Yankees, Canadiens and Celtics have nothing on Ludwig van Beethoven. Since the mid-19th century, Beethoven has been the dominant figure in concert music. Brahms was haunted by him, Bruckner worshiped him, and Wagner was inspired by him. Pianists, string quartets and symphony orchestras perform his music incessantly, and audiences never tire of it. In the nearly 180 years since his death, Beethoven has fended off all contenders to World's Greatest Composer and shows no signs of losing his title."

Friedrich Nietzsche, by Edvard Munch, 1905

Willful Philosopher: 1844-1900

THOUGH HE'S FAMOUS FOR KILL-ing God, Friedrich Nietzsche did a much better job of killing truth. Everything after him—even good and evil—is just perception. He did to philosophy what quantum physics would do to the physical world 40 years later. Thanks to Nietzsche, we have existentialism, nihilism, deconstructionism and, therefore, cafés.

Part of the thrill of reading Nietzsche is that you *can* read Nietzsche. He writes in aphorisms, or what we now call tweets. (Two different Nietzsche feeds, in fact, have more than 10,000 Twitter followers.) Nietzsche is the only philosopher I've ever read who is legitimately funny. He's also clear—none of that lawyer talk that makes Immanuel Kant's *Prolegomena to Any Future Metaphysics That Will Be Able to Present Itself as a Science* so impenetrable. (Kant has only 559 Twitter followers.) Instead of spending 50 pages trying to prove the existence of a table, Nietzsche talks in staccato bursts about the stuff of life: ethics, progress, relationships, keeping an open mind. He is a self-help motivator as much as a philosopher.

Or, as he put it more succinctly: "In individuals, insanity is rare; but in groups, parties, nations and epochs, it is the rule."

Because his ideas are still so radical—he dismisses Judeo-Christian ethics as a ploy for the weak to seize power from the strong—they've been used for both good and evil. Though Nietzsche was a firm antinationalist and hater of anti-Semitism who dismissed the politics of his musical hero, Richard Wagner, in two books, Adolph Hitler used some of his aphorisms. Jerry Siegel and Joe Shuster drew on Nietzsche's *Ubermensch* when they named Superman. Those who seek to shoot Nietzsche down always mention that he had a mental breakdown when he saw a horse being whipped and threw his arms around it to protect it (he was seriously sick, plus he was right about the treatment of the horse).

But no one can deny that by dismissing more than 2,000 years of moral assumptions, he opened up the world to radical new ways of thinking. So he cried over a horse. Even Superman is vulnerable to kryptonite.

—By Joel Stein

Friedrich Nietzsche

Louis Armstrong

Trailblazing Musician: 1901-1971

POPS. SWEET PAPA DIP. SATCHMO. He had perfect pitch and perfect rhythm. He was a small man, but the extent of his influence across jazz, across American music and around the world has continuing stature; he supplied revolutionary language that took on such pervasiveness that it became commonplace, like the light bulb, the airplane, the telephone.

He grew up poor, hustling and hustling. Yet his world was not dominated by the deprivation of poverty but by the ceremonial vigor of the Negroes of New Orleans and their music: rags, blues, snippets from opera, church music and whatever else. At the Colored Waifs' Home, young Louis first put his lips to the mouthpiece of a cornet; soon he was formidable. Musicians then were wont to have "cutting sessions"—battles of imagination and stamina. From 1920 on, young Louis was hell on two feet if somebody challenged him.

Fairly soon, he was left alone. He took his music to Chicago, then to New York City, where his improvised melodies and singing set the city on its head. The stiff rhythms of the time were slashed away by his combination of the percussive and the soaring. His combination of virtuosity, strength and passion was unprecedented. No one in Western music—not even Bach—has ever set the innovative pace on an instrument , then stood up to sing and converted the vocalists. He did.

Apollo and Dionysus met in the sweating container of a genius from New Orleans whose sensitivity and passion were epic in completely new terms. He bent and twisted pop songs until they were shorn of sentimentality and elevated to serious art. He brought the change agent of swing to the world, the most revolutionary rhythm of the 20th century. Pops. Sweet Papa Dip. Satchmo.

—By Stanley Crouch

Primal, Protean Artist: 1881-1973

BEFORE HIS 50TH BIRTHDAY, Pablo Picasso had become the very prototype of the modern artist as public figure. The little Spaniard from Málaga and his work were the subjects of unending analysis, gossip, dislike, adoration and rumor. He was the Minotaur in a canvas-and-paper labyrinth of his own construction.

There was scarcely a 20th century movement that he didn't inspire, contribute to or—in the case of Cubism, which he co-invented with Georges Braque—beget. Much of the story of modern sculpture is bound up with welding and assembling images from sheet metal, rather than modeling in clay, casting in bronze or carving in wood; this tradition arose from one small guitar that Picasso snipped and joined out of tin in 1912. Collage, the gluing of previously unrelated things and images on a flat surface, became a basic mode of modern art, due to Picasso's Cubist collaboration with Braque. He was never a Surrealist, but in the 1920s and '30s he produced some of the scariest distortions of the human body and the most violently irrational, erotic images of Eros and Thanatos ever committed to canvas. He was not a realist, and yet *Guernica* remains the most powerful political image in modern art.

Long before any Pop artists were born, Picasso latched on to the magnetism of mass culture and how high art could refresh itself through common vernaculars. He then went to the opposite extreme of embracing the classical past with his painting of huge dropsical women dreaming Mediterranean dreams. He became the artist with whom virtually every other artist had to reckon.

—*By Robert Hughes*

Pablo Picasso

Master Form-Giver: 1886-1969

THIS IS LUDWIG MIES VAN DER Rohe's world; we just live in it. The master of Modernist architecture was one of the single most powerful influences on the look of the 20th century. It was Mies and his fellow architects from Germany's innovative Bauhaus School, strongly influenced by the visionary American architect Frank Lloyd Wright, who created the forward-looking designs that put a definitive end to the long reign of Andrea Palladio. "The age demanded an image/ Of its accelerated grimace," declared poet Ezra Pound, and in the streamlined forms, glass curtain walls and severe geometries of the Modernist architects, the 20th century found its most fitting expression in design.

When Hitler's policies forced the nation's best architects into exile, Mies came to the U.S. in 1937 and found a home at today's Illinois Institute of Technology in Chicago, the great city of the skyscraper. Famously arguing that "less is more," Mies took an Occam's razor to the elaborately ornate Beaux Arts styles that flourished at the end of the 19th century and deployed new technologies in glass and steel to strip away complex exterior embellishment and reveal the infrastructure of buildings with surprising grace.

At its best, the new style produced light, airy structures of astonishing clarity, elegance and integrity, like Manhattan's Seagram Building, which seems to levitate somewhere above the plaza on which it rests. When it was opened in 1958, this soaring tower of glass gleamed like a postcard from the future amid its clunky, stone-faced neighbors along New York City's Park Avenue. At its worst, knock-off Modernism ignored Mies van der Rohe's minatory injunction—"God is in the details"—and reduced buildings to plain, unadorned boxes, devoid of style and grace and appealing primarily to clients focusing on the bottom line. Don't blame Mies for these.

All clear? *Mies designed Crown Hall for the campus of the Illinois Institute of Technology in 1954*

Ring leader *Ali sizes up opponent Joe Frazier during the 1975 "Thrilla in Manila"*

Muhammad Ali

Iconic Athlete: 1942-

FEW HUMAN BEINGS HAVE BEEN so deified in their own time. Then again, few humans have spent so much of their own time deifying themselves. "I am the greatest!" Muhammad Ali often declared—and eventually, most people came around to share his view. Born Cassius Clay in Louisville, Ky., he was a prankster from childhood, and merriment always seemed to be bubbling just below his surface, sweetening his braggadocio with just the right amount of sugar. After earning fame by winning the gold medal in light-heavyweight boxing at the Rome Olympics in 1960, he rose quickly to the top of the pro ranks, prancing and dancing in the ring as no boxer ever had before, yet able to throw and take punches of terrific force.

By 1964, the "Louisville Lip" was the world champ. A modern-day P.T. Barnum, Clay had reached into boxing's then tawdry backroom and dragged his sport back into the limelight, laughing all the way. But there was more to Clay than the amusing rhymes and the silly pranks, as Americans soon discovered: that year he declared himself a member of the Nation of Islam, a controversial movement that sought to empower African Americans, christening himself Muhammad Ali.

Many Americans now denounced the brash boxer as a radical, and he was even more widely vilified when he refused to join the Army as the Vietnam War escalated. "I ain't got no quarrel with them Viet Cong" he memorably declared. He was found guilty of refusing induction into the service in 1967, and the boxing commission quickly revoked his license to fight; the U.S. Supreme Court reversed that decision in 1971.

Ali was idle for more than three years when he was at the height of his powers. Yet when he returned, he expressed no bitterness, and he still had the old magic. He won back the title in 1974 by knocking out George Foreman in their fight in Zaïre—the "Rumble in the Jungle." Another international bout, the 1975 "Thrilla in Manila," in which he beat Joe Frazier, helped Ali become the best-known person on the planet—and, it seemed, the most beloved. In later years, his uncomplaining battle with Parkinson's Disease further cemented his status as a global icon of courage, grace and good will.

Musical Innovators: 1960-70

SELDOM HAVE THE AGENTS OF cultural change arrived with such explosive impact. When the Beatles began topping the charts in Britain in 1963, then conquered the U.S. in early 1964, they dazzled us with their buoyant spirits, their bottomless charm and irrepressible wit. Their overflowing gifts for songcraft, harmony and instrumental excitement, their bright quips and their ready smiles made them appear almost otherworldly: Planet Earth just wasn't prepared to handle this much fun.

If they had stopped there, they would have been a delightful footnote to history. But the Fab Four won a place in this book by refusing to settle for being pop stars: they considered themselves artists and made the music to prove it. Exhausted by touring, they walked away from live performing. Retreating to their famed creative lair, the EMI Studios at Abbey Road, they secluded themselves with their full partner, producer George Martin, and created a run of albums unmatched for brilliance, power, range and innovation: *Revolver, Sgt. Pepper, The White Album, Abbey Road.*

The four Brits from Liverpool transformed rock 'n' roll from teen dance music into rock: a full-fledged, vital new art form that changed the world as surely as did Louis Armstrong's take on jazz. Shunning others' work, they insisted on writing their own songs, a radical departure in pop music. They became cultural avatars as well, leading an entire generation, for better and worse, into experiments with drugs and encounters with Eastern spirituality, Pop Art and confrontational politics.

As a group, they were far stronger than their individual parts, reaping the benefits of mutual creativity. They seemed one being at times. John Lennon was the mind: brilliant, satirical and scathing. Paul McCartney was the heart: mushy to a fault (and by far their finest musician). George Harrison was the soul, leading their investigation of Indian music and culture. And Ringo Starr—well, he was the body, the world's luckiest Everyman. It was too good to last, and the group separated seven years after Beatlemania first kicked in. In the meantime, they reinvented our culture—with a beat you could dance to.

The Beatles

Other Shapers of Culture
Three writers exerted influence far beyond the page

J.W. von Goethe
1749-1832

Johann Wolfgang von Goethe was a notable philosopher, a crack professional scientist, a successful bureaucrat, a stylist second to none in German literature, a major novelist and dramatist and probably the most richly expressive lyric poet who ever lived—a genius who differed in kind but not in degree from Dante and Shakespeare. He wrote a hundred times more than either of them—his collected works fill 150 volumes—and consequently more of what he wrote is dated; *The Sorrows of Young Werther* (1774), for instance, reads in this unsentimental age like soap opera written on steroids.

Goethe's finest works—*Iphigenia in Taurus, Tasso, Elective Affinities*—embrace a wide range of experience, and in them all the print still lies warm on the page. The drama *Faust* is a masterpiece more than 60 years in the making in which Goethe presents a central image of Western civilization and limns a hero who is the template of modern man.

Charles Dickens
1812-70

Ebenezer Scrooge and Mr. Micawber. David Copperfield and Oliver Twist. Miss Havisham and Tiny Tim. The characters created by Charles Dickens still endure, second only to those of Shakespeare in their blend of exaggerated caricature and convincing realism. Dickens, a man of prodigious energies and enthusiasms, pushed back against a hardscrabble childhood and rose to become the most popular storyteller of his time. His fictions, published in serial form, enchanted the world.

Dickens could have coasted on his brilliant gift for characterization and cliff-hangers. But he challenged himself, emerging as a powerful critic of Victorian society, a role he furthered as a magazine and newspaper editor. In such works as *Bleak House, Hard Times* and *Dombey and Son,* he trained his critical, unerring gaze on social ills and hypocrisies, while his popular series of Christmas books helped invent our modern observance of the holiday.

Leo Tolstoy
1828-1910

Today Leo Tolstoy is admired for his two towering, realistic novels, *War and Peace* (1869) and *Anna Karenina* (1875). But in his day, Tolstoy also provoked the world with his pronouncements on politics and art, Christianity and charity. The wealthy nobleman who inherited an estate outside Moscow and earned fame for his journalistic reporting on the Crimean War became an outspoken social critic and activist whose views won legions of sympathizers in prerevolutionary Russia. Then, changing gears again, he embraced a vigorous form of Christianity, renounced his art and became a sort of secular prophet, one who influenced both Mohandas Gandhi and Martin Luther King Jr.

A master of fiction who scorned art, a nobleman who yearned to be a peasant, a preacher of humility who considered himself only once removed from Christ, Tolstoy was a conflicted genius who could make searing self-rebuke seem gluttonous.

Commentary

From 100 to Eternity

By Joel Stein

EVERY YEAR TIME MAGAZINE COMPILES A list of the 100 most influential people in the world at that moment, which teaches its readers many things. Shallow things about this brief moment in history, but, still, things. But I knew that some readers—in particular the intellectuals and strivers out there—would be more interested in a list I put together online of the 100 most influential people in history. The All-Time TIME 100 of All Time™ was a list designed not just to make you think, like the regular TIME 100, or even to make you think about thinking, like you thought I was going to say, but to make you think about how smart I am.

To make the All-Time TIME 100 of All Time™ list, I followed several rules that seem to govern the TIME 100. There had to be a lot more Americans than are historically warranted, I had to pile on as many minorities and women as possible, and I had to prove that some influential people are attractive movie stars. Also, I had to contact a brain trust of experts so that I could point to them if questioned about any of my choices.

The first expert I called was James Lipton, host of Bravo's *Inside the Actors Studio.* Normally, when conducting an interview, you have to ask at least one question, but Lipton started with Euripides and kept talking for 45 minutes. He confidently eliminated whole swaths of history, saying things like, "The Romans don't make it for me." Along with picking Shakespeare, Mozart and Beethoven, Lipton had some surprising choices, such as George Balanchine and Stephen Sondheim. For actors he chose Edmund Kean and Charlie Chaplin. Then he said, "For a 20th century actor, should we say it together? One, two, three …" I said, "Brando!" while he said, "Brahhhhhndo." I never nail that say-it-at-the-same-time thing. At least this time I didn't blurt out, "I love you." Though I almost did.

Lipton's list was great, but it was full of white men. For help I called Cornel West, a professor at Princeton's Center for African-American Studies and author of *Brother West: Living and Loving Out Loud,* but the voice mail he left me was less list-broadening than I'd hoped. "Brother Joel Stein, hope you're staying strong," he said. "Don't forget St. Francis of Assisi and Martin Luther King Jr.

Definitely Chekhov. I'd say John Coltrane." Then he tried to come up with some women: "I wish it were Toni Morrison. I'd probably say Antigone, but she's not for real." One thing was clear: Cornel West will never host *Inside the Actors Studio.*

When I asked historian Douglas Brinkley for a bunch of Americans I could plausibly shove on the All-Time TIME 100 of All Time™, he started pouring them out: George Washington, Abraham Lincoln, Thomas Edison, Walt Whitman, Elvis Presley, the Wright Brothers, Neil Armstrong. He was really good at this. He told me that was because he was writing a preface for a book about the 100 most influential people in history. A book being put out by TIME. This book. Which I didn't know about.

I couldn't believe that TIME's book division was brazenly stealing my totally original All-Time TIME 100 of All Time™ idea. So I called Steve Koepp, my old editor, who now supervises TIME Books, and asked him whether, after nine years, TIME had run out of ways to exploit the TIME 100 or I had run out of ways to make fun of it. Before we could figure that out, we started comparing our lists. The All-Time TIME 100 of All Time™ (which you can read at *time.com/joelslist*) was so obviously better. His list had just three people whose last name was "the Great." Mine has 15. I'm pretty sure that if someone gets called the Great, it's for a reason, like that they're great. His list has no actors, while mine has four, and he doesn't have a single celebrity chef. And he doesn't have anyone who became famous in this millennium, whereas I have Mark Zuckerberg, which greatly increases the odds of my list being posted all over Facebook.

While I was in the midst of mocking him (Abraham wasn't a real person! Ashoka the Great was no Cyrus the Great! You didn't talk to James Lipton!), Koepp told me his list wasn't finalized and he'd take mine into consideration. Plus, I could write one of the entries. As I worked on the Nietzsche page, I realized that the TIME 100 is less a silly gimmick than a wonderful intellectual parlor game, which is a phrase I've heard the editors of TIME use since 1999 and which I have used to make fun of the editors of TIME since 1999. But now that I've finally been included, I am way into intellectual parlor games. I can't wait to be invited to more of them. Maybe a night of six degrees of Bernard-Henri Lévy or an appearance in a Ken Burns documentary. I can't believe I ever made fun of these lists in the first place. ∎

Joel Stein is a TIME *columnist. This essay appeared in slightly different form in the 2012* TIME 100 *issue, dated 4/30/2012.*

TIME

MANAGING EDITOR Richard Stengel
ART DIRECTOR D.W. Pine
DIRECTOR OF PHOTOGRAPHY Kira Pollack

The 100 Most Influential People of All Time

EDITOR Kelly Knauer
DESIGNER Ellen Fanning
PICTURE EDITOR Patricia Cadley
RESEARCH Tresa McBee
COPY EDITOR Bruce Christopher Carr

TIME HOME ENTERTAINMENT

PUBLISHER Richard Fraiman
VICE PRESIDENT, BUSINESS DEVELOPMENT AND STRATEGY Steven Sandonato
EXECUTIVE DIRECTOR, MARKETING SERVICES Carol Pittard
EXECUTIVE DIRECTOR, RETAIL AND SPECIAL SALES Tom Mifsud
EXECUTIVE PUBLISHING DIRECTOR Joy Butts
DIRECTOR, BOOKAZINE DEVELOPMENT AND MARKETING Laura Adam
FINANCE DIRECTOR Glenn Buonocore
ASSISTANT GENERAL COUNSEL Helen Wan
ASSISTANT DIRECTOR, SPECIAL SALES Ilene Schreider
BOOK PRODUCTION MANAGER Suzanne Janso
DESIGN AND PREPRESS MANAGER Anne-Michelle Gallero
BRAND MANAGER Michela Wilde
ASSOCIATE BRAND MANAGER Isata Yansaneh
ASSOCIATE PREPRESS MANAGER Alex Voznesenskiy

EDITORIAL DIRECTOR Stephen Koepp
EDITORIAL OPERATIONS DIRECTOR Michael Q. Bullerdick

SPECIAL THANKS
Christine Austin, Jeremy Biloon, Jim Childs, Susan Chodakiewicz, Rose Cirrincione, Lauren Hall Clark, Brian Fellows, Jacqueline Fitzgerald, Christine Font, Jenna Goldberg, Hillary Hirsch, Amy Mangus, Robert Marasco, Kimberly Marshall, Amy Migliaccio, Nina Mistry, Dave Rozzelle, Adriana Tierno, TIME Imaging, Vanessa Wu

ISBN 13: 978-1-60320-997-7 ISBN 10: 1-60320-997-2
Library of Congress Control Number: 2012931013

We welcome your comments and suggestions about TIME Books. Please write to us at: TIME Books, Attention: Book Editors, P.O. Box 11016, Des Moines, IA 50336-1016

To order any of our hardcover Collector's Edition books, please call us at 1-800-327-6388. Hours: Monday through Friday, 7 a.m.–8 p.m., or Saturday, 7 a.m.–6 p.m., Central Time

Contributors

William Lee Adams (*Machiavelli*) *is a writer in the London bureau of* TIME.

Howard Chua-Eoan (*Genghis Khan*) *is the news director for* TIME *and* Time.com.

Stanley Crouch (*Armstrong*) *is a noted critic and novelist. His* Considering Genius: Writings on Jazz *was published in 2007.*

Bill Gates (*Wright Brothers*), *the co-founder and chairman of Microsoft, is a co-founder of the Bill and Melinda Gates Foundation.*

Peter Gay (*Freud*) *is the Sterling Professor of History Emeritus at Yale University. His study* Modernism: The Lure of Heresy *was published in 2007.*

Lev Grossman (*Babbage*), *a writer and book critic for* TIME, *is the author of* The Magician King: A Novel (*2012*).

Robert Hughes (*Columbus, Leonardo, Palladio, Rembrandt, Picasso*) *is the former art critic for* TIME *and author of* Rome: A Cultural, Visual and Personal History (*2011*).

Walter Isaacson (*Einstein, Watson and Crick*), *the president and CEO of the Aspen Institute, is the former managing editor of* TIME *and the author of* Steve Jobs (*2011*).

John Keegan (*Churchill*) *is a noted military historian and author. His* The American Civil War: A Military History *was published in 2009.*

Johanna McGeary (*Queen Elizabeth I*), *is a veteran* TIME *writer and editor, now retired.*

Lance Morrow (*Newton, Jefferson*), *a longtime writer for* TIME, *is retired. His* Second Drafts of History *was published in 2006.*

Sherwin B. Nuland (*Hippocrates*) *is a writer and professor at the Yale School of Medicine.*

Christopher Porterfield (*Bach*), *a veteran* TIME *writer and editor, is now retired.*

David Remnick (*Lenin*) *is editor of the* New Yorker *and author of* The Bridge: The Life and Rise of Barack Obama (*2010*).

Joel Stein (*Nietzsche*) *is a columnist at* TIME. *His* Man Made: A Stupid Quest for Masculinity, *was published in 2012.*

Gloria Steinem (*Sanger*) *is an activist, journalist and commentator. Her* Doing Sixty and Seventy *was published in 2006.*

Marina Warner (*Pankhurst*) *is a professor at the University of Essex and fiction writer. Her* Stranger Magic: Charmed States and the Arabian Nights *was published in 2011.*

Photography Credits

FRONT COVER: Clockwise from top left: (Lincoln) Alexander Gardner—Library of Congress Prints and Photographs Division; (Mother Teresa) Tim Graham—Getty Images; (Jobs) Alan Levenson—Corbis Outline; (Mandela) Louise Gubb—Corbis Saba; (Christ) Painting by Giotto di Bondone—Universal Images Group—Getty Images; (King) Flip Schulke—Corbis; (Beethoven) Painting by August Klober—Universal History Archive—Getty Images; (Sanger) Bettmann—Corbis; (Gandhi) Hulton-Deutsch Collection—Corbis; (Michelangelo) Painting by Giuliano Bugiardini—Photo by Scala—Art Resource, NY; (Beatles) Harry Hammond—V&A Images—Getty Images; (Gutenberg) Painting by Jean-Antoine Laurent—Photo by Gianni Dagli Orti—The Art Archive—Art Resource, NY; (Einstein) Eliot Elisofon—Time Life Pictures; (Darwin) English Heritage, National Monuments Record, Great Britain—HIP—Art Resource, NY; (Roosevelt:) George Skadding—Time Life Pictures; (Queen Elizabeth I) Painting by John Bettes the Younger—The Bridgeman Art Library

BACK COVER: (Pericles) Photo by Dea G. Nimatallah—De Agostini—Getty Images; (Joan of Arc) Painting by Sir John Everett Millais—Photo by Peter Nahum at The Leicester Galleries, London—Bridgeman Art Library; (Shakespeare) The "Cobbe Portrait"—Unknown Artist—Corbis; (Sitting Bull) Corbis

FRONT MATTER: i Clockwise from top left: Einstein photo by Popperfoto—Getty Images; James L. Dick copy of 1805 Rembrandt Peale portrait of Thomas Jefferson—Monticello—Thomas Jefferson Foundation Inc.; *Life of Christ* Fresco detail by Giotto di Bondone—Photoservice Electa—Universal Images Group—Getty Images; Queen Elizabeth I Portrait by George Peter Alexander Healy after Marcus Gerards the Younger—Réunion des Musées Nationaux—Art Resource, NY. iii Arnold Newman—Getty Images. 1 Washington's Life Mask by Jean-Antoine Houdon—The Pierpont Morgan Library—Art Resource, NY

BEACONS OF THE SPIRIT: 2 (left) Rubin Museum of Art—Art Resource, NY; Catacomb of Priscilla, Rome, Italy—Photo by Erich Lessing—Art Resource, NY. 3 (left) Collection Isaac Einhorn—Italy—Photo by Erich Lessing—Art Resource, NY; Sarcophagus of the Muses—Musée du Louvre, Paris—Photo by Gianni Dagli Orti—The Art Archive at Art Resource, NY. 4 Painting by Lelio Orsi—Photo by Scala—Ministero per i Beni e le Attivita Culturali—Art Resource, NY. 5 British Library, London—HIP—Art Resource, NY. 6 Paul Chesley—National Geographic—Getty Images. 8 Painting by Jacques Louis David—Photo ©The Metropolitan Museum of Art—Art Resource, NY. 9 1st Century A.D. Mosaic—Photo by Alfredo Dagli Orti—The Art Archive—Corbis. 10 Frescos by Giotto di Bondone (4) (clockwise from top left) Photo by Mauro Magliani—Alinari—Art Resource, NY; Photo by Scala—Art Resource, NY; Photo by Cameraphoto Arte, Venice—Art Resource, NY (2). 12 *Conversion of St. Paul*—Niedersächsisches Museum—The Art Archive at Art Resource, NY. 13 Mohammed Abed—AFP—Getty Images. 14 Photo by Anatoly Pronin—Art Resource, NY. 15 (left) Artist Unknown—Photo by Alfredo Dagli Orti—The Art Archive—Art Resource, NY; K.M. Westerman—Corbis. 16 Painting by Giotto di Bondone—Photo by Alfredo Dagli Orti—Art Resource, NY. 17 Drawing by Hans Veit Schnorr—Bettmann—Corbis. 18 Raghu Rai—Magnum Photos. 19 (left to right) Illustration from book by Edward T.C. Werner—Private Collection—The Bridgeman Art Library; Painting by Pedro Berruguete—Photo by Scala—Art Resource, NY; James L.

Stanfield—National Geographic—Getty Images.

EXPLORERS AND VISIONARIES: 20 (left) SSPL—Getty Images; British Library, London—HIP—Art Resource, NY. 21 (left) Biblioteca Estense, Modena, Italy—Photo by Scala—Art Resource, NY; Science Picture Co.—Science Faction. 22 Bust of Hippocrates—Louvre, Paris—Photo by Erich Lessing—Art Resource, NY. 23 (left) Hand-Coloured Woodcut circa 1754—Photo by Universal History Archive—Getty Images; Frontispiece of 17th Century Edition of *Elements of Geometry*—Universal History Archive—Getty Images. 24 Detail of Painting *The School of Athens* by Raphael—The Bridgeman Art Library—Getty Images. 25 Painting of Aristotle with a Bust of Homer by Rembrandt—Photo by Metropolitan Museum of Art—Corbis. 26 no credit. 27 British Library, London—HIP—Art Resource, NY. 28 William James Warren—Science Faction—Corbis. 29 Painting from Polish School—Bridgeman Art Library—Getty Images. 30 Engraving after Theodor de Bry—The Bridgeman Art Library. 31 Painting by Anonymous, 16th Century—Photo from Scala—White Images—Art Resource, NY. 32 Painting by Jean-Antoine Laurent—Photo by Gianni Dagli Orti—The Art Archive—Art Resource, NY. 33 Painting by Felix Farra—Photo by Gianni Dagli Orti—The Art Archive—Art Resource, NY. 34 (left) Painting by Sébastien Bourdon—Photo by Erich Lessing—Art Resource, NY; Painting by Sir James Thornhill—The Gallery Collection—Corbis. 35 Edgar Samuel Paxson—Peter Newark American Pictures—Bridgeman Art Library. 36 Tui De Roy—Minden Pictures. 37 Julia Margaret Cameron—Stapleton Collection—Corbis. 38 Corbis. 39 FPG—Archive Photos—Getty Images (2). 40 SSPL—Getty Images (2). 41 Hulton-Deutsch Collection—Corbis; Time and Life Pictures. 42 Adoc Photos—Art Resource, NY. 43 Eliot Elisofon—Time Life Pictures. 44 Bettmann—Corbis. 45 Bettmann—Corbis. 46 Bettmann—Corbis. 47 A. Barrington Brown—Photo Researchers. 48 Alan Levenson—Corbis Outine. 49 (from left) Yadid Levy—Robert Harding World Imagery—Corbis; Fresco by Antonio Giovanni de Varese—Photo by Gianni Dagli Orti—The Art Archive—Art Resource, NY; Bettmann—Corbis.

LEADERS OF THE PEOPLE: 50 (left) Hoberman Collection—Corbis; Currier and Ives—Library of Congress Prints and Photographs Division. 51 (left) Sandro Vannini—Corbis; Macduff Everton—Corbis. 52 Tapestry *The Exodus* by Marc Chagall—Photo by Bridgeman-Giraudon—Art Resource, NY—©Artists Rights Society (ARS) New York/ADAGP, Paris. 54 (left) Photo by Dea G. Nimatallah—De Agostini—Getty Images; Hulton Archive—Getty Images. 55 Photo by Gianni Dagli Orti—The Art Archive—Art Resource, NY. 56 Photo by Dea Picture Library—De Agostini—Getty Images. 57 Photo by Eric Vandeville—Gamma-Rapho—Getty Images. 58 BPK, Berlin—Staatliche Museen—Art Resource, NY. 59 Axiom Photographic—Design Pics—Corbis. 60 Engraving by V. Raineri—The Bridgeman Art Library. 61 Bridgeman-Giraudon—Art Resource, NY. 62 Painting by Cristofano dell'Altissimo—Scala—Ministero per i Beni e le Attivita Culturali—Art Resource, NY. 63 National Palace Museum—The Gallery Collection—Corbis. 64 Isidore Patrois—Musée des Beaux-Arts, Rouen, Frankreich—Getty Images. 66 Copy after Juan de Flandes—Photo by Erich Lessing—Art Resource, NY. 67 From Copy of *Codex Tlaxcala*—Photo by Gianni Dagli Orti—The Art Archive at Art Resource, NY. 68 Artist Unknown—Photo from The Gallery Collection—Corbis Images. 69 (left) Painting by Lucas Cranach the Elder—The Bridgeman Art Library; Mansell Collection—Time Life Pictures. 70 (left) Painting by Guillaume Scrots—The Bridgeman Art Library; Artist Unknown—The Gallery

Collection—Corbis Images. 71 (left) Painting by John Bettes the Younger—The Bridgeman Art Library; Artist Unknown—The Bridgeman Art Library. 72 Painting by Fyodor Alekseyev—Photo by Scala—Art Resource, NY; (inset) Painting by Jean-Marc Nattier—Imagno Collection—Hulton Archive—Getty Images. 73 Life Mask by Jean-Antoine Houdon—The Pierpont Morgan Library—Art Resource, NY. 74 Painting by Alfred Francois Mouillard—Bridgeman-Giraudon—Art Resource, NY. 75 Painting by John Keenan—The Bridgeman Art Library. 76 Jacques Louis David—Photo by Erich Lessing—Art Resource, NY. 78 Fernando Leal—Photo by Gianni Dagli Orti—The Art Archive at Art Resource, NY. 79 Corbis. 80 Alexander Gardner—Library of Congress. 82 Mansell Collection—Time Life Pictures. 83 Buyenlarge—Getty Images. 84 Time Life Picture Collection. 85 Bettmann—Corbis. 86 Hugo Jaeger—Time Life Pictures. 87 Bettmann—Corbis. 88 Bettmann—Corbis. 89 Photo by Hulton Archive—Getty Images. 90 Hulton-Deutsch Collection—Corbis. 91 Leonard Freed—Magnum Photos. 92 Louise Gubb—Corbis Saba. 93 (left to right) Photo by Gianni Dagli Orti—The Art Archive at Art Resource, NY; Artist Unknown—Photo by Tim Graham—Alamy; AFP—Getty Images.

ARCHITECTS OF CULTURE: 94 (left) Self-Portrait by Pablo Picasso—The Gallery Collection—Corbis, ©2012 Estate of Pablo Picasso/Artists Rights Society (ARS), New York; *Vitruvian Man* by Leonardo da Vinci—Bettmann Corbis. 95 (left) Alexandre-Gabriel Decamps—The Gallery Collection—Corbis; Michael Ochs Archives—Corbis. 96 (left) Photo by Araldo de Luca—Corbis; (inset) The Bridgeman Art Library—Getty Images. 97 Vanni—Art Resource, NY. 98 Photo by Erich Lessing—Art Resource, NY. 99 Fresco by Domenico di Michelino (detail)—Photo by Erich Lessing—Art Resource, NY. 100 *Atlantic Codex*—Photo by Dea—Veneranda Biblioteca Ambrosiana—Art Resource, NY. 101 Self-Portrait by Leonardo da Vinci—Photo by Alinari—Art Resource, NY. 102 Bust by Antonio del Pollaiolo—Photo by Arte & Immagini SRL—Corbis. 103 Painting by Giuliano Bugiardini—Photo by Scala—Art Resource, NY. 104 Private Collection—The Bridgeman Art Library. 105 (left) Engraving—Photo by Hulton Archive—Getty Images; Juan de Jáuregui y Aguilar—Private Collection—Bridgeman Art Library. 106 The "Cobbe Portrait"—Unknown Artist—Corbis. 107 Self-Portrait by Rembrandt van Rijn—Photo by Corbis. 108 (left) Painting by Elias Gottlieb Haussmann—Photo by Erich Lessing—Art Resource, NY; The Pierpont Morgan Library—Art Resource, NY. 109 Painting by Benjamin West—Philadelphia Museum of Art—Corbis. 110 Erich Lessing—Art Resource, NY. 111 Engraving by Charon—Photo by Gianni Dagli Orti—The Art Archive at Art Resource, NY. 112 Mount Rushmore Memorial by Gutzon Borglum—Photo by Bettmann Corbis. 114 Universal History Group—Getty Images. 115 Edvard Munch—Photo by Dea-M. Carrieri—De Agostini—Getty Images—© 2012 The Munch Museum/The Munch-Ellingsen Group/ Artists Rights Society (ARS), NY. 116 Hulton-Deutsch Collection—Corbis. 117 Herbert List—Magnum Photos. 118 Arthur Siegel—Time Life Pictures—Getty Images. 119 Neil Leifer—Sports Illustrated. 120 Robert Whitaker—Getty Images. 121 (left to right) Johan H. Tischbein—Photo by Gianni Dagli Orti—The Art Archive at Art Resource, NY; Herbert Watkins—Rischgitz—Getty Images; Adoc Photos—Art Resource, NY.